An account of the
Leicestershire village of Earl Shilton,
together with the neighbouring parishes
of Kirkby Mallory and Elmesthorpe,
in the nineteenth century

Lady Byron
and Earl Shilton

Lady ByronThe Rev. F. E. Tower

By David Herbert

ACKNOWLEDGEMENTS

My Family - My wife, Sheilah. Ruth and Andrew Hammond, Rebecca and Bryony. Their assistance with word processing, checking and typing proved invaluable.

The Earl and Countess of Lytton for permission to use material from Lady Byron's personal papers deposited in the Bodleian Library, Oxford. Also for their valued friendship over many years. Likewise to our mutual friends Peggy and Desmond Aldridge.

The Bodleian Library, Oxford, and particularly Mrs. Mary Clapinson, Keeper of Western Manuscripts, for providing access to the *"Lovelace Byron papers"*.

Mr. Bernard Beatty, of the Dept. of English Language and Literature, The University of Liverpool, for some invaluable professional guidance.

Miss Meriel Tower for family information, and photographs of the Tower family and F. W. Robertson.

Mr. Ken Purslow, Mrs. Maureen Crisp, Terry and Marion Needham of the Newstead Abbey Byron Society for their encouragement and interest in the project.

Ms. Angela Cutting of the Living History Unit, Mr. Malcolm Clayson and Ms. Kim Pereira of Creativity Works (Leicester City Council) for their interest and technical assistance in the publication.

Mrs. Haidee Jackson, Keeper of Newstead Abbey, for her personal interest and help with information when required.

Mr. John Gilbert, Mr. Joe Lawrance, Mrs. Rosemary Coe, Mr. Bryan Wills, Mr. John Reilly, Phillip Lindley, Hugh Beavin and Sidney and Marian Herbert who have all helped in some way in bringing this book to completion.

To Sheilah, Ruth, Neil, Dianne, Andrew, Steve, Rebecca, Bryony, Daniel, Samantha and Benjamin.

Published by Hinckley and District Museum Ltd.
Framework Knitters' Cottages,
Lower Bond Street, Hinckley,
Leicestershire. LE10 1QX
Registered Charity no. 1015922

Printed by Chartwell Press, Leicester
© A.D.Herbert 1997
ISBN 0 9521471 3 0

Index

Foreword	by the Countess of Lytton	5
Introduction		7
Chapter One	The Noels of Kirkby Mallory	11
Chapter Two	Lord Byron	19
Chapter Three	Lady Byron takes Control	31
Chapter Four	The Rev John Longhurst and Mr Charles Noel 1825-53	37
Chapter Five	The Rev. Frederick William Robertson	51
Chapter Six	The Rev. Ferdinand Ernest Tower and the Earl Shilton Transition	61
Chapter Seven	Lady Byron - The Last Decade	79
Chapter Eight	The "New" Earl Shilton	93
Appendix A	The Byron - Tower Legacy	109
Appendix B	A Guide to Earl Shilton Church	121

Note:

When quoting from old letters, which of course were hand-written, I have in a very few instances had to guess at certain words which I could not decipher but this in no way alters the meaning of the letter. I have also made adjustments to the spelling in a few instances, particularly to the village name of ELMESTHORPE where even in official documents it is often spelt ELMSTHORPE. Words such as 'favor' or 'honorable' I have left as written. Where a dotted line appears I have left out a sentence or paragraph which is irrelevant. Letters between Lady Byron, Charles Noel and Ernest Tower are taken from the Lovelace Papers now catalogued as the *Lovelace Byron Papers* at the Bodleian Library, Oxford. The ancestry of the Baker Tower family I discovered in Durham Record Office, with additional information from Miss Meriel Tower. Where information has been obtained from newspapers and magazines this has been shown in the text.

The Proceeds from the sale of this book are for charitable purposes.

Photographs and Illustrations

1 Lady Byron 8
2 Lady Judith Noel 10
3 Sir Edward Noel, 1st Viscount Wentworth 12
4 Judith, Lady Wentworth, wife of 1st Viscount Wentworth 13
5 Thomas Noel, 2nd Viscount Wentworth 17
6 George Gordon - 6th Lord Byron 30
7 The Rev Thomas Noel, absentee Rector 32
8 Sir Francis Burdett 33
9 Kirkby Mallory Hall 36
10 Peckleton House 39
11 Earl Shilton Parish Church 1790 49
12 The Rev Frederick William Robertson 55
13 The Rev Ferdinand Ernest Tower 60
14 Ada, Countess of Lovelace 78
15 Deed of the Manor of Earl Shilton to Lady Byron 81
16 Sampler - worked by Evelena Rowley Foster 82
17 Inscription on monument to Ada at Kirkby Mallory 86
18 J.Toon & Sons Ltd. - Earl Shilton factories 90
19 Hon and Rev. Augustus Byron, Rector of Kirkby Mallory 94
20 Tower's concert programme 97
21 Mrs Mary Georgina Tower 98
22 The Tower Family, with Domestic Staff, at Earl Shilton vicarage 99
23 The Tower Family at Mrs.Tower's grave 99
24 Plan of Earl Shilton Parish Church 122
25 Earl Shilton's Rebuilt Parish Church 127

The Portraits of the 1st Viscount and Lady Wentworth are by Thomas Hudson and are reproduced by kind permission of Leicester City Museums Service. The portrait of Lady Judith Noel is by James Northcote. The sampler worked by Miss Foster is reproduced by kind permission of Leicester City Museums Service. The Deed of the Manor of Earl Shilton is reproduced by kind permission of the Earl of Lytton and the Bodleian Library, Oxford dept. Lovelace Byron 234 Item 1. The portrait of Lord Byron is by Thomas Phillips and is reproduced by kind permission of City of Nottingham Museums; Newstead Abbey. Other portraits are from the author's collection, and from Mrs Peggy Aldridge.

FOREWORD
by the Countess of Lytton

Sometimes a historian is criticised for producing a record of the privileged named few at the expense of the anonymous many. David Herbert will not face such censure; his history of Earl Shilton at the time of Lady Byron gives identity to many underprivileged inhabitants of his home village at a fascinating, though difficult and turbulent time.

His research shows Lady Byron as a responsible and caring landowner, rather than the unhappy young wife and anxious mother more usually described at the time of the separation from her famous poet husband. She deals tactfully with her Noel cousins, chooses her advisers wisely and - what is more - let them get on with the job without interference. With the benefit of hindsight, her idea of finding a suitable clergyman and financing him and his projects to alleviate the destitution of Earl Shilton may seem an obvious solution for a wealthy well-intentioned Christian landowner.

However, I suspect that her task of finding a remedy for the ills of a rapidly changing society was no easier then than it is today. All those interested in history, both in its local and wider context, will enjoy this carefully researched book.

Newbuildings Place
July 1997

INTRODUCTION
Lady Byron and Earl Shilton

I have wanted to write this book for a number of reasons. It is surprising that no one locally in the last century thought it worthwhile to write down for posterity an eyewitness account of those fascinating but difficult times. It has however been a most enjoyable task for me to search through archive material in The Bodleian Library at Oxford and The Leicestershire Record Office and other sources to recreate some of the major events which took place.

This is mainly a work of local history based on primary sources and presenting unpublished information about the large industrial Leicestershire village of Earl Shilton. However, as Lady Byron is closely involved with this local history, my book takes on another perspective.

Lady Byron is known mainly through the biography of her famous husband but in these pages we see her in a different context. To understand her fully it is necessary to know what 'ordinary' people felt for her and how she in turn treated her tenants and all those to some extent dependent on her.

The book should therefore be of interest to those who have some connection with Earl Shilton, and to all those who are interested in the life and times of the poet, the 6th Lord Byron.

Those who have read some of the hundreds of books on Byron cannot fail to have gained a bad impression of his estranged wife. I found that what I had read contradicted my local knowledge of her and this is a reason I felt the book may be found useful. I am not concerned with who was right or wrong in the context of the marriage and separation but rather to look at Lady Byron as an individual.

I do have to declare an interest. My paternal grandmother was born on 1st

January 1860, in Earl Shilton, just a few months before Lady Byron died on 16th May. She died in 1937 when I was eighteen months old. My father told me how she spent several weeks in the Hinckley Workhouse in 1862 with her family as a result of the cotton famine. She knew the Rev. Tower, but sadly I shall never know in detail her personal recollections of that period. Her father, my great grandfather, was a framework knitter born in 1816 and he would have experienced some of the events set out in this book personally, but, alas, very few personal recollections have been handed down. It is understandable that they should want to forget, as we shall see.

Byron as man and poet is perennially interesting. There are particular reasons for our present sympathy with him. He was brought up in a one parent family, was handicapped with a deformed right foot, suffered sexual abuse, encountered bullying at school. The local connection, of course adds interest to the subject. I believe him to be the most fascinating Englishman of all time. It is interesting to speculate as to what might have been, had the Byron marriage not broken up and the couple had then chosen to live at Kirkby Mallory Hall. It must be emphasised that the poet Byron never came to Kirkby Mallory or Earl Shilton for as we shall see steps were taken to prevent this happening.

The book also serves as a tribute to the villagers of Earl Shilton in the early and middle period of the last century who endured so much hardship and misery. Poverty affected almost every family on a scale that is unknown today and charity was for some the only means of survival. Lack of leadership aggravated by an absentee Rector made matters worse.

I have put together this book from information gathered over the past thirty years. I feel that it is quite likely there is other interesting material waiting to be discovered in newspapers and documents relating to Earl Shilton and perhaps sometime in the future someone may have the pleasure and reward of seeking this out.

Finally of course it is important to record the part that Lady Byron and Ernest Tower played in the transformation of the village, so that it will be remembered by future generations. Also this area's connection with the world famous poet and his talented daughter, Ada, whose work is now acknowledged by the computer industry, should never be forgotten. I hope that the reader will find it as interesting to read as I have found it most rewarding to research and write.

Left: Lady Byron – wife of the poet the 6th Lord Byron

Judith, Lady Byron's mother. She was the daughter of the 1st Viscount Wentworth. On her marriage she became Mrs Milbanke and later Lady Milbanke. In 1815 after inheriting the Kirkby estates from her brother, she became Lady Noel.

CHAPTER ONE

The Noels of Kirkby Mallory

The Noel family can trace their ancestry back to Norman times and their connections with Kirkby Mallory came about with the marriage of a younger son, John Noel to Anne Fowler of Elmesthorpe.

John Noel's father was Andrew Noel of Dalby who was Sheriff of Rutland during the reign of Henry VIII. John's elder brother, Andrew, inherited his father's estates and became the ancestor of the Noel line who were created Earls of Gainsborough, but John inherited sufficient funds to enable him to contract the marriage to Anne Fowler herself an heiress with estates which included property at Elmesthorpe, Kirkby Mallory, Peckleton and Earl Shilton; all these villages being within three miles of each other about ten miles south west of Leicester.

During the English Civil War the estates passed to Verney Noel who married a sister of Wolstan Dixie of Market Bosworth thus further expanding the Noel influence in this part of Leicestershire. Verney Noel and Wolstan Dixie both supported the Royalists in the war and upon the restoration of the monarchy in 1660 were created baronets.

Sir Verney Noel's son and heir William married in 1660 Margaret, daughter of Lord Lovelace of Hurley, further enhancing the standing of the family. Their great grandson Sir Edward Noel (1715-1774) married Judith, daughter of William Lamb in 1744 and through various deaths and childless marriages in related families he succeeded to the title of 9th Baron Wentworth in 1745. This year was to prove a special year for the new Baron Wentworth as his son and heir Thomas Noel was born on 18th November 1745.

Three daughters were then born; Judith in 1751, Elizabeth in 1755 and Sophia in 1758. Lady Wentworth died in 1761 and Wentworth was fortunate in having an unmarried sister, Mary Noel, about ten years his junior who then lived with the family at Kirkby and readily took on the responsibility of running

Sir Edward Noel,
!st Viscount Wentworth

the household and bringing up the children which she did with love and affection.

Wentworth had also two brothers who were both clergymen. The younger of the two named Rowney (his name was taken from his mother's maiden name) was Rector of Kirkby Mallory with Earl Shilton and also Rector of Elmesthorpe. He was known as the Rev. Doctor Noel and it is worth recording here that with the enclosures taking place in Earl Shilton in 1778 the enclosure map shows him holding land off Hinckley Road. This is how the name 'Doctors Fields' (well known to residents of Earl Shilton) came into being. In 1780 he was appointed Dean of Salisbury and thereafter was referred to as 'the Dean'. His wife was Maria, daughter of Thomas Boothby Skrymsher of Tooley Park and sister of the infamous Charles Boothby Skrymsher, often referred to as Prince Boothby, because of his extravagant lifestyle, one of his followers being the dandy Beau Brummel. Prince Boothby shot himself in the year 1800 it is said because he was simply tired of getting up and dressing each morning and undressing again in the evening. The enclosure map shows him as owner of much land in Earl Shilton which he subsequently sold.

It was in the 1760's that Dr Noel was inducted into the living of Elmesthorpe and it was during his incumbency that the roof of the church fell in. The building was then used as a garden and as a pen for cattle. Dr Noel, however, refused to allow stone from the church to be taken away and used for road building as was often the practice in those days when each parish was responsible for the maintenance of roads in its area.

Judith, wife of the 1st Viscount Wentworth

The 9th Baron Wentworth was further rewarded with a promotion to the rank of Viscount becoming the 1st Viscount Wentworth of Wellesborough in 1762. Wentworth's name appears as one of those persons who actively supported the founding of the Leicester Royal Infirmary. He was chairman of the committee which met at the (Three) Cranes Inn at Leicester on 17th August 1768 to decide from the many plans submitted the one that should be proceeded with for the design and building of the Infirmary. He attended a further twelve meetings of the committee and was chairman at six of these prior to the official opening on 11th September 1771. At a meeting also held at the (Three) Cranes Inn on 5th July 1771, Lord Wentworth is shown as being a vice-president. He is again shown as chairman at a committee meeting on 18th June 1772.

A church service was held, to commemorate the first anniversary of the opening, on 25th September 1772. The sermon on this occasion was preached by his youngest brother Dr Rowney Noel. Lord Wentworth took the chair for the last time at a meeting which followed this service. Meanwhile his son Thomas had completed his formal education at Eton and Oxford University and as was usual for young men in his position he undertook the Grand Tour of Europe. Soon after his return, his father's health became a matter for concern, and in spite of consultations with many of the best doctors of the day, and a visit to Bath to take the waters, he died of cancer in 1774 just before his sixtieth birthday. He was buried at Kirkby Mallory alongside his late wife.

Before his thirtieth birthday Thomas Noel now became 2nd Viscount

Wentworth and succeeded to the Kirkby Mallory and other estates with his seat at Kirkby Mallory Hall. Still living at the Hall was his unmarried aunt Mary and his three young sisters now aged twenty four, nineteen and sixteen. His uncle Rowney was nearby at the Rectory. Marriage at this time was often a means of bringing two noble families together with benefits accruing from financial arrangements set out in the contracts drawn up by the lawyers representing each party. In spite of such legal necessities the new Lord Wentworth's three sisters were all married in the year 1777.

The youngest Sophia married The Hon. Nathaniel Curzon, son and heir of Lord Scarsdale of Kedleston Hall in Derbyshire. This marriage produced two children, a daughter named Sophia after her mother in 1779 and a son named Nathaniel after his father in 1781. The marriage was not a particularly happy one and Sophia after suffering many health problems died in 1782. Her portrait hangs at Kedleston Hall.

Elizabeth married James Bland Burges an ambitious young man who was to become a lawyer and Member of Parliament. The marriage lasted only two years before Elizabeth died as a result of complications in pregnancy in 1779.

The eldest sister Judith married Ralph Milbanke and in contrast to her two sisters the marriage was to last forty-five years until her death in 1822. The marriage took place on 9th January 1777 at Kirkby Mallory Church and was performed by Judith's uncle Rowney, the Rector. The Milbanke family were landowners in the north east of England with estates at Halnaby Hall in North Yorkshire and Seaham in County Durham. The marriage remained childless until 1792 when Judith was forty years of age although the Milbankes did look after Sophia Curzon after the death of her mother, Judith's sister. This was an extremely happy marriage and the couple lived life to the full. Much of their time was devoted to civic affairs and visiting neighbouring estates where they played cards, danced, wined and dined. They visited the races too, and enjoyed sea bathing and visiting fashionable spas to take the waters. They also took part in national affairs with Ralph becoming M.P. for County Durham in 1790. He was later to support William Wilberforce in his cause to abolish slavery. Judith, clearly the dominant partner in this marriage, made use of every opportunity to further her husband's career. The couple made many visits to Kirkby to see Lord Wentworth and to meet many family friends. Judith was also keen to keep an eye on her brother.

Lord Wentworth continued his father's interest in the Leicester Royal

Infirmary and was elected a vice-president and was also a trustee. He took the chair at many meetings of the committee between 1781 and 1811. Just before his father's death he was elected M.P. for the County of Leicester but was forced to resign on succeeding to the peerage. A few weeks later, in November 1774, he took his seat in the House of Lords.

From the 1750's the history of the Noel family is recorded in hundreds of letters and documents sent and received by various members of the family. These documents are now catalogued as the *Lovelace Byron Papers*. As well as telling us intimate details of the family, they are historically important for they give eye witness accounts of the day to day events in the country.

Lord Wentworth appears to have been a very amiable person. He carried out his duties in the locality and in London attending the House of Lords and becoming a Lord of the bed-chamber in the Royal Household. The records show his associations with the other great families of the area:- The Dixies of Market Bosworth, The Boothby Skrymshers of Tooley Park, Clement Winstanley of Braunstone Hall, Edward Yeo of Normanton Park who was M.P. for Coventry, Charles Loraine Smith of Enderby Hall, The Earl of Denbigh of Newnham Paddox and many more. Like most lords of his time he ate and drank too much and he gambled away part of his inheritance, but fortunately he reformed in time to keep his estates together. In 1788 at the age of 42 he married Mary, Countess Ligonier, a widow, but no children came about from this marriage. He did, however, have two illegitimate children by his mistress, Catherine Vanloo, a daughter named Anna and a son, another Thomas Noel born in 1775. This Thomas Noel was to become Rector of Kirkby Mallory and to live until August 1853. It was not until his death that the parishes of Earl Shilton and Elmesthorpe could become independent of Kirkby Mallory - we will return to this later. In 1802 he followed the example of his great uncle Dr Rowney Noel by preaching at the anniversary service of the Leicester Royal Infirmary.

During the conflict with Napoleon many local volunteer forces were formed in the early 1800's and the force which was raised from the Earl Shilton, Kirkby Mallory and Hinckley areas trained at Kirkby Mallory Hall under the command of Lord Wentworth. On his death in April 1815 the *Gentleman's Magazine* referred to him as 'One of the most polite and accomplished noblemen of the age, possessed of a very superior knowledge of the classics - a most generous landlord and to his domestics and the poor a worthy and liberal friend'. At this time his bailiff was a John Lynes whose family had held the position for many years. In his Will, Wentworth made provision for his two illegitimate children, but the bulk of the estate passed to his sister Judith Milbanke then living at Seaham in County Durham. She and her husband, now Sir Ralph following the death of his father, were obliged by the terms of the Will to change their names to Noel.

Lady Judith and Sir Ralph left the north east to reside at Kirkby Mallory and it appears that Judith did not like what she saw. Suspecting Lynes of mismanaging the estates, she replaced him with her own steward from the north east, John Davison. A notice appeared in the *Leicester Journal* on 25th August 1815 as follows 'Manors of Kirkby Mallory, Peckleton, Desford, Elmesthorpe, Barwell, Stapleton and Wellesborough in the County of Leicester having been trespassed upon by unqualified persons, shooting and otherwise destroying the Game. This is to give notice that persons are appointed to lodge information against all such trespassers by order of the Hon. Lady Noel and poachers will be prosecuted with the utmost vigour of the law - Kirkby Mallory, 23rd August 1815.'

It is noticeable that Earl Shilton does not appear in this list. Following the Enclosure Act of 1778 the Noels held almost no land in the village, and it was rapidly becoming a large industrial area. Whereas the villages mentioned in the notice had large landowners who controlled expansion Earl Shilton did not, and without leadership the population was, according to reports, out of control. It does serve to emphasise how different were the origins of the parishes of Earl Shilton and Kirkby Mallory. In the Middle Ages, Earl Shilton belonged to the Earls of Leicester and its history was closely connected with the City of Leicester, Leicester Forest and Tooley Park. Tooley Park was in fact known as Shilton Park when the castle next to the church was in use by the Earl. The forest and the village passed to the Earls of Lancaster who took over the land after the defeat of Simon de Montfort, Earl of Leicester. When John of Gaunt died in 1399 and his son became Henry IV in that year Earl Shilton belonged to the Crown. The importance of Earl Shilton, along with the City of Leicester and Leicester Forest, declined from this date. During the following two hundred years the church and the living at Earl Shilton became a chapelry of Kirkby Mallory probably for convenience. The Noels had replaced the Mallorys as the principal family in the area during this time and their influence was to determine events in Earl Shilton up to 1853 and beyond.

Sometime before Lady Judith's notice in the newspaper a meeting had been called on 2nd June 1815 of the Kirkby Mallory Association at the White Buck Inn at Kirkby Mallory, the notice of the meeting being signed by Thomas Fulshaw, Treasurer. Quite likely this was called at Judith's request to consider the implications of the new order. Further notices appeared giving details of the sale of farm implements which indicates the new approach being taken. Lady Judith however was not enjoying good health; she was now 63, had been seriously ill, and was under the care of some of the most celebrated doctors of the time.

Thomas Noel, 2nd Viscount Wentworth

Lady Judith also encountered problems in meeting the terms of the Will providing for Anna and Thomas. She was forced to sell land and property held by the trustees at a time when prices were very depressed following the Napoleonic troubles and Thomas Noel became increasingly hostile towards Judith and her family resulting in lawsuits.

After his father's death in April 1815, Thomas's presence at Kirkby Mallory was very infrequent if at all and he ceased to carry out his duties as Rector. This is confirmed by the fact that his name no longer appears in the church registers of baptisms. His duties were carried out by a curate the Rev. Henry Pemble and by others. If the parish of Kirkby Mallory suffered by his absence then the effect on Earl Shilton was to be even worse.

Judith was to live at Kirkby for about seven years dying on 28th January 1822 at the age of seventy. The direct family connection with Kirkby Mallory would then come to an end, although descendants would still have an interest in the village for many years to come. She was a remarkable woman, a matriarchal figure who controlled her husband and brother in such a way as to enhance the families' interests and defend them against outsiders. She was a fine horsewoman and an excellent shot. She was friendly with members of the Royal Family and many of the influential families of the time. She was also a friend of Mrs Sarah Siddons, the actress. Fortunately for posterity she was an excellent letter writer who preserved nearly all of the family letters.

As we have seen, Judith's marriage to Ralph Milbanke was childless until she reached the age of forty, when a daughter was born on 17th May 1792 to the surprise and delight of the family. At this time Judith's new house on the cliffs at Seaham was being built and the daughter was born at the house of her friends Mr & Mrs George Baker of Elemore Hall nearby. She was named Anne after her godmother the Duchess of Cumberland, and Isabella after Mrs Baker, but the two Christian names soon became merged and from an early age she was known as Annabella.

Annabella, adored by her parents, grew up in the beautiful new house at Seaham. She had a nurse, a Mrs Clermont, who was to stay with the Milbankes to see Annabella reach adulthood. She assisted in her education and watched over her through the usual childhood illnesses. In addition to the academic subjects Annabella studied music (her father played the violin and her mother the piano) dancing and poetry and with Mrs Clermont she designed and made ladies' shoes. These would be the fabric ones as worn by ladies at that time.

Judith presided over the locality in much the same way as she did over her own family. Estate workers received education, and medical help, and other assistance with problems they would encounter. This upbringing was to prepare Annabella for her adult life in the type of society in which her mother had been such an outstanding success. But life in the more remote parts of the north east was very different to that which she would encounter in Regency London.

All young ladies of her standing were introduced to London Society in their teenage years and in 1811 at the age of nineteen Annabella was in London. She had one particular advantage as her aunt, Elizabeth, Lady Melbourne, her father's sister, was one of the most fashionable hostesses in London. It was to Melbourne House that she stayed which provided her with an ideal base for meeting all the eligible young men of the time. This lifestyle was not to Annabella's liking and as soon as possible she was back in her beloved Seaham having rejected a number of suitors including Augustus Foster, son of the Duchess of Devonshire by her first marriage. In 1812 she was back in London but this time she was to meet the most famous poet of the day, Lord Byron, and things would never be the same again.

CHAPTER TWO

Lord Byron

The life of Lord Byron is very well known, and hundreds of biographies exist, but we will need to remind the reader of its outline here. George Gordon Byron was born in Holles Street, London, near to Oxford Street, on 22nd. January 1788. His father was known as 'Mad Jack' Byron, not without good reason, as scandal of one sort or another followed him through life. He first married Lady Carmarthen with whom he had a daughter, Augusta, in 1784. Within a few years he had disposed of his wife's sizeable fortune and was soon heavily in debt and spending a lot of time in France to escape his creditors. Following the death of Lady Carmarthen he was to use his considerable charm to gain another heiress for his wife. Where better to look than fashionable Bath? The lady who quickly succumbed to his calculated charm was Catherine Gordon of Gight, a Scottish heiress. This union produced the boy who was to become the poet. Soon however her fortune had gone and his creditors were in pursuit once again.

In 1791 Jack Byron died penniless at the age of thirty-six. The widow with her three year old child had little alternative but to return to her native Scotland, to Aberdeen. Byron was to live there until he was ten years old in 1798.

The 5th. Lord Byron, known as the 'Wicked Lord' died at his home, Newstead Abbey, in Nottinghamshire during that year and following the early death of the 5th. Lord's grandson a few years earlier, the young Byron inherited the title and estates. Now the 6th. Lord Byron, the ten year old boy with his mother travelled down to Nottinghamshire but sadly the Abbey and the estate had been neglected and the family were forced to live in neighbouring Nottingham and Southwell. He received treatment for a deformed right foot while in Nottingham without much success, and later went to school at Harrow and then to Trinity College, Cambridge. Life was never dull when Byron was around and his tutors and fellow students had already marked him out as possessing very special talents which manifested themselves in his general lifestyle and in particular in his use of words.

1812 was to be the year that, to his surprise, he awoke one morning and found himself famous, but first he was to take a two - year journey around Europe with his friend John Cam Hobhouse. This journey influenced him greatly resulting in his lifelong love of Greece and the classical world, which he had read about at Harrow. He had written the first two cantos of his poem 'Childe Harold' based on his travels and it was the publication of this poem that made him the literary giant in fashionable London. Everyone wanted to read it and to meet the now famous poet was a priority.

Lady Melbourne, Annabella's aunt, was to invite Byron to her very fashionable house parties which was to lead to much anguish over the next few years. Two young ladies in particular were to have their lives changed forever, Annabella and Lady Melbourne's daughter-in-law Lady Caroline Lamb. The former was to have a disastrous marriage to him on 2nd. January 1815 and the latter, already married to Lady Melbourne's son William, later to become Queen Victoria's first Prime Minister, was so besotted with him that she resorted to all sorts of antics to try to win his affections.

By the time of the marriage of Byron and Annabella things had so cooled between them that it was doomed to failure. Volumes have been written about the happenings in this year of 1815 as to the behaviour of the couple with numerous writers giving their interpretation of events and trying to allocate blame. For the purpose of this book it is sufficient to say that Thomas 2nd. Viscount Wentworth died in April and as mentioned in the previous chapter Annabella's parents moved to Kirkby Mallory Hall, and secondly that on 10th. December a daughter Augusta Ada was born to Lady Byron in London.

When Ada, as she was to be called, was just over a month old on 15th. January 1816 it was decided that Annabella, or Lady Byron as we shall now call her, should go with Ada to stay with her parents at Kirkby Mallory. Byron, it seems, was to follow but as it was to turn out he was never to see his wife and child again. From January to April 1816 Kirkby Mallory Hall was to be the centre of activity relating to the separation with Judith, now Lady Noel, conducting negotiations with lawyers and collating evidence as to Byron's conduct from friends and acquaintances. Any contact with Byron was made through Sir Ralph.

Among those who told Lady Noel of Byron's alleged outrageous behaviour was Lady Caroline Lamb who took great pleasure in getting her revenge on Byron for being rejected. The view was taken that Byron must be unstable if not bordering on insanity. Lady Byron was now forced to take a back seat and follow the instructions of her lawyers, particularly Dr. Stephen Lushington who was to become a lifelong friend.

It must be remembered that Lady Noel had lived most of her life in the eighteenth century and she believed in great families owning and administering great estates and contracting marriages with other noble families to enhance their mutual status. She no doubt had many talks with her brother Lord Wentworth to ensure that Annabella succeeded to the Kirkby Estates and the opinions which she formed of Byron did not fit her image of a responsible husband for her daughter and she was not going to see all that she had so carefully planned for thrown away. It is said locally that the various lodges at the entrances to Kirkby Park were guarded and the residents put on the alert and armed should Byron try to invade and steal his daughter. In those days it was more likely that Byron could have claimed custody of the child and it was partly for this reason that Ada was made a Ward of Chancery.

With the odds stacked against him Byron finally signed a deed of separation and on 23rd. April 1816 he set sail from Dover for the continent never to return to these shores again during his lifetime. His parting gift to his wife was a poem entitled 'Fare Thee Well!' which is printed at the end of this chapter together with two poems said to have been written by Lady Byron in response.

Byron's life was to continue for just another eight years, dying in his beloved Greece on Easter Monday 19th April 1824 serving the cause of Greek independence. In these eight years he travelled through Belgium, Germany and spent the summer of 1816 in a villa overlooking Lake Geneva in Switzerland. In this historic setting he met up with the poet Shelley and his wife Mary who had a villa nearby. This gathering produced the now well known horror story of 'Frankenstein' written by Mary, and Byron's 'The Prisoner of Chillon' written after a visit to the Chateau of the same name. The magnificence of the Alps inspired other great poems such as 'Manfred'. Here, too, he continued with his quasi - epic poem 'Childe Harold'.

Byron was now so famous throughout Europe that wherever he went he became the object of curiosity and interest. Telescopes were used to try and see him from the lake and all manner of rumour and exaggerated stories circulated. His reputation was such that a Mrs. Hervey (aged 65) fainted on seeing him entering a room and Lady Liddell, a friend of the Noel family, told her daughter to look away as it was dangerous to make eye contact with him. These stories seem hard to take in but they occurred, and indeed a Mrs. Opie writing for the *Leicester Journal* as late as 1857 said 'His voice was such a voice as the devil tempted Eve with, you feared its fascinations the moment you heard it'

The years 1817 to 1823 were spent in Italy, where he gave his support to local freedom fighters, causing the authorities to be wary of his presence. The company of mistresses, visits to classical sites, and poetry and writing occupying most of his time. Finally it was as if he was called by fate to make his final journey to Greece and particularly to the town of Missolonghi where he was to die. Byron's death was to make him a hero in Greece and his influence throughout Europe reached statesmen, politicians, freedom fighters, writers, musicians and artists alike. Even to this day his name is used to support a variety of special causes. A proposal to build recently in Harrow was objected to partly on the grounds that it would spoil the views and images enshrined in some of his poems. On the local scene Byron's death was to have an impact on events in Kirkby Mallory and Earl Shilton as we shall see in the next chapter, but first here is the satirical poem written by Byron before leaving England. This poem is very well known but it is followed by two rarely printed poems said to have been written by Lady Byron in response:

Lord Byron's poem published just before he left England for good in 1816, addressed to Lady Byron

Fare thee well! and if for ever,
Still for ever, fare thee well:
Even though unforgiving, never
'Gainst thee shall my heart rebel.

Would that breast were bared before thee
Where thy head so oft hath lain,
While that placid sleep came o'er thee
Which thou ne'er canst know again;

Would that breast, by thee glanced over,
Every inmost thought could show!
Then thou wouldst at last discover
'Twas not well to spurn it so.

Though the world for this commend thee-
Though it smile upon the blow,
Even its praises must offend thee,
Founded on another's woe;

Though my many faults defaced me,
Could no other arm be found,
Than the one which once embraced me,
To inflict a cureless wound?

Yet, oh yet, thyself deceive not;
Love may sink by slow decay,
But by sudden wrench, believe not
Hearts can thus be torn away:

Still thine own its life retaineth,
Still must mine, though bleeding, beat;
And the undying thought which paineth
Is - that we no more may meet.

These are words of deeper sorrow
Than the wail above the dead;
Both shall live, but every morrow
Wake us from a widow'd bed.

And when thou wouldst solace gather,
When our child's first accents flow,
Wilt thou teach her to say 'Father!'
Though his care she must forego?

When her little hands shall press thee,
When her lip to thine is press'd,
Think of him whose prayer shall bless thee,
Think of him thy love had bless'd!

Should her lineaments resemble
Those thou never more may'st see,
Then thy heart will softly tremble
With a pulse yet true to me.

All my faults perchance thou knowest,
All my madness none can know;
All my hopes, where'er thou goest,
Wither, yet with thee they go.

Every feeling hath been shaken;
Pride, which not a world could bow,
Bows to thee-by thee forsaken,
Even my soul forsakes me now:

But 'tis done - all words are idle -
Words from me are vainer still;
But the thoughts we cannot bridle
Force their way without the will.

Fare thee well! thus disunited,
Torn from every nearer tie,
Sear'd in heart, and lone, and blighted,
More than this I scarce can die.

Lady Byron's responsive 'Fare Thee Well' printed by Richard Edwards, Crane Court, Fleet Street, London - 29th April 1816. (Written whilst she was living at Kirkby Mallory)

And fare Thee well too - if for ever-
How dread the thought! - still fare thee well!
Yet think not time or space can sever
The heart that wont on thine to dwell!

O cherish not the sad illusion,
All thy high-wrought hopes deceiving,
Which whispers thee, THAT heart's profusion
Of love can end in 'unforgiving!'

Too well I know thy conscious breast,
That form'd, how brief! my 'placid' pillow,
Hath wander'd from its ark of rest,
Far stretching o'er life's cheerless billow:

But if - as may - peace still denied thee-
My bosom beat to thy return-
The love that once hath dar'd to chide thee,
Cannot - will not - dare to 'spurn'.

THOU wert MY world - another 'world'
Scatters its frowns or smiles in vain!
From thy embrace by treachery hurl'd,
I know no joy, I fear no pain.

To soft affection's duties prone,
In me thy thoughts a veil had found:
Thy 'many faults' were thine alone-
NOT THINE ALONE their 'cureless wound'.

This lesson thou hadst fix'd too deep,
Ere yet thy verse display'd its art-
The sudden deluge cannot sweep
Love's graven impress from the heart!

But oh! if mine 'by slow decay'
Must moulder from its ruby throne,
Thy hand shall wear the stamp away-
For yet my love is all thine own!

And oft as on my 'widow'd bed'
The light revisits these sad eyes,
Anguish more deep than for the dead
Is foster'd by unbidden sighs.

When first our infant's vocal aim
With skill distinctive shall be crown'd-
When taught to lisp a father's name,
Embitter'd joy will greet the sound:

For then-should still thy footsteps wander
Far from her who mourns thee lost-
Then on her griefs recall'd she'll ponder,
On all her joys so foully cross'd.

And if one gleam of 'solace' cheer me,
Flickering o'er my gloomy fate-
My lord, my love, no longer near me -
Nought left of him beside his hate-

'Twill be, that Nature's pencil true
Shall on our darling's cherub cheek
Those thrice dear 'lineaments' renew,
Her mother else might vainly seek!

'Twill be, that if her face resemble
Thine, which I never more may see-
While gazing there my heart may tremble
With a pulse still true to thee!

Again thy 'faults!'- but hadst thou known,
Ere yet too late, thy slighted peace;
Thy wither'd 'hopes' -and oh! my own-
Had flourish'd with our years' increase!

With me - 'with thee' - they sever'd fly,
Cherish'd alone by dear communion;
Without me - without thee - they die
Beneath their violated union.

Thy 'pride', thy ev'ry other 'feeling',
These self-condemned faults have 'shaken;'
And if beyond the power of healing,-
By me! - no - by THYSELF 'forsaken!'

Haply from me hath Nature banish'd
The flames that feed thy cherish'd 'madness'-
Enough for me to 'know' is vanish'd
Ev'ry glimpse of future gladness.

And whence emerge the baleful streams
That soil'd the promise once so fair,
Whelming all our blissful dreams
In the black chaos of despair?

'Tis not relentless Virtue's hand
Hath rent the torrent's faithless mound:-
Welcome again her whispers bland,
And exil'd love shall yet be found.

For oh! might one repentant tear
But tremble on thy blanched cheek;
I'll bless the sacred record there,
Nor other trophy dare to seek.

Might but the radiant bow of peace
Rise in the heaven of thine eye;
Each boding fear, each doubt shall cease,
And all my woes forgotten die.

But if it must be - fare thee well!
If to thy bosom death can give
No deeper wound - mine throbs to tell,
Its more than dying is - to live!

Lady Byron's Farewell to her husband as printed in the *'Leicester Journal'*;

Fare thee well, O youth mistaken,
A long adieu to love and thee;
The heart thou hast so oft forsaken
Has burst its trammels and is free.

The loveliest and most fragrant flower
Withers beneath the chilling blast,
Loses it's beauty every hour,
Then drops its head and dies at last.

The flame of love will burn forever
When nurs'd by fond affection's art,
When life expires they die together
Together leave the human heart.

But when neglect each way assails it
When insult seeks to quench its fires,
Though it may struggle what avails it?
It languishes and then expires.

No transient glance has hovered over
The saddest prospect of thy breast;
I have read it, and discover
There the grave of all my rest.

Oft shall I mourn extinguish'd passion
Oft dwell on hours for ever flown,
Shall view thy frailties with compassion,
And all thy matchless talent own.

What pity that a mind so gifted
Should thus to pattern be resigned,
Like some fair vessel rudely drifted
Without a rudder by each wind.

What pity that when fortune showers
A thousand blessings on thine head,
Thus to quit thy nobler powers
And thus be hoodwinked, thus misled.

The poet's wreath that has adorn'd thee
Withers at thy late misdeeds,
And many a virtuous heart has scorn'd thee
Knowing mine with anguish bleeds.

Hads't thou known that heart's dread sorrow
Ere it received the final blow;
How it attempted hope to borrow
And struggled to escape from woe;

Pity then had conquered passion
And nature's favourite child restrain'd,
And if not love, at least compassion,
A victory for us both had gain'd.

Say not the arms that have caress'd thee
No pity on thy breast has shown;
She would have still as fondly press'd thee
Had I believed that heart mine own

That tender pledge of soft affection
Shall oft a mother's tears receive,
Shall oft revive fond recollection
And make me for her father grieve.

For him her voice shall lisp in prayer,
Together shall unite our songs;
Thou shalt her best affections share
Untainted by a mother's wrongs.

Perhaps our mutual prayers ascending
May pardon for thine errors done;
Oh! that our hopes and wishes blending
May not ascend to heaven in vain!

Then fare thee well, once husband, lover,
When pleasure's voice has lost her charms,
When the gay giddy dream is over,
How thou will shun the wanton's arms?

Once more farewell, and may kind heaven
Bestow its richest gifts on thee;
And may free pardon thence be given
As that which thou receives from me.

Lady Byron, before her marriage, had read some of Jane Austen's novels including *Pride and Prejudice*. It can be said that she did not exercise the same caution over her marriage to Byron that Elizabeth Bennett did with Mr. Darcy. Though one is fact and the other fiction there is great similarity between the two events. The year 1813 was both the year of publication of *Pride and Prejudice* and the first proposal of Byron. Did Lady Byron see herself in the role of Elizabeth Bennett? Did she see Lord Byron as the handsome, talented though unpredictable Mr. Darcy? Could she influence his wayward lifestyle and live happily thereafter? Did Byron believe that the marriage was an escape route from his troubles and the attention of his many female admirers?

George Gordon, 6th Lord Byron

CHAPTER THREE

Lady Byron takes Control

Following the separation, Lady Byron with Ada made her home at Kirkby Mallory Hall often leaving the child with her very loving grandparents while she visited friends in other parts of the country. Grandmother Judith enjoyed having little Ada around and this was perhaps as well as Lady Byron was able to prepare for her future life as a single parent under her mother's guidance.

Although Byron was now out of sight he was not out of mind and rumour and recrimination abounded. Byron's sister Augusta, at first welcomed to Kirkby, was now regarded as being partly responsible for what had happened. Byron and Augusta were very close and Byron made no secret of his affection for her in his letters and poetry, and he even suggested that she might join him on the continent. Incest was a suspicion already broadcast by Lady Caroline Lamb.

Lady Byron herself now became an object of curiosity. Small crowds were eager to catch sight of her wherever she travelled. She visited her old home at Seaham and crossed the border into Scotland to visit (Sir) Walter Scott who had met Byron and admired his poetry.

On 2nd. November 1816 Ada, just before her first birthday, was received into Kirkby Mallory Church and the entry recorded in the Register of Baptisms. The register records that the ceremony was performed by the Rev. Pemble who notes that she was first baptised on 20th. December 1815 at St. Georges, Hanover Square by the Rev. Thomas Noel. Apparently this procedure was not unusual in those days when because of infant mortality a short quick ceremony was held as soon as possible after birth.

Ada did her schooling at Kirkby Hall under a governess. She also had a nurse to look after her through the usual childhood illnesses. Grandmother

The Rev. Thomas Noel, the absentee Rector

Judith finally died on 28th. January 1822 and was buried at Kirkby Mallory.

The Kirkby estates were now vested in Lord Byron and his wife both having an equal share. Byron at first planned to return to England to attend to these matters but in the end settled to leave Sir Francis Burdett, a well known Leicestershire fox hunting squire, to look after his interests. Sir Francis was a radical and had been jailed for his anti-government views. This appealed to Byron who in 1812 had made his maiden speech in the House of Lords against the proposed introduction of the death penalty for framebreakers. Sir Francis called it 'the best speech by a Lord since the Lord knows when!'

In her will Judith gave specific instructions regarding a portrait of Byron which she had acquired some years earlier. This may have been the famous portrait of Byron in Albanian costume by Phillips. It effectively meant that it was to remain in its case and could not be viewed by Ada until she reached maturity. Other portraits which are known to have hung at Kirkby Mallory Hall at that time were the full length portraits of the 1st. Viscount and Lady Wentworth by Thomas Hudson subsequently sold and then repurchased by Leicester Museum in the 1940's. For a time they hung on the staircase at Belgrave Hall, Leicester, but during the refurbishment of the Hall in the 1980's were put into store. There was also a portrait by Tilly Kettle of the 2nd. Viscount Wentworth with his three sisters. He and Sir Ralph were painted by Sir Joshua Reynolds and Judith by Northcote.

Following Judith's death Lord and Lady Byron, though separated, had to add the name Noel to their surnames in order to comply with the terms of the inheritance, and this caused some amusement to Byron as it gave him the same initials as Napoleon Bonaparte who had been his hero. It was no coincidence that Byron was probably the most well known person in Europe after Napoleon.

For the next thirty years a serious situation was to develop over the parishes of Kirkby Mallory with Earl Shilton and Elmesthorpe. With the Rev. Thomas Noel absent but having no intention of resigning as Rector there was very little that Lady Byron, now patroness of the living, could do to remedy the situation. He had been appointed to this office by his father and could in effect remain as Rector for the rest of his life, which is just what he did. In fact he tried to take matters further by communicating directly with Lord Byron soon after Judith's death in 1822 to the effect that should he die the living ought to be offered to one of his sons, probably his eldest son also named Thomas, who was born in 1799. Byron could not understand the request thinking it was for the father whom he knew had the living already or it concerned some other living.

Fortunately Byron had the good sense to leave matters to Lady Byron who was well aware of what a promise to do so would mean to the locality. Byron was sympathetic to Thomas Noel since he had conducted the wedding ceremony at Seaham Hall in 1815. He felt that but for his illegitimacy he would have become 3rd. Viscount Wentworth on the death of his father and the total inheritance would then have passed to him. As it was the title lapsed. Indeed for the local parishes it may also have been of great benefit for Thomas to have succeeded to the title and estates because they probably would not have been so neglected in the coming years. Things did not work out that way and Thomas was to be an absentee Rector for nearly forty years.

Sir Francis Burdett

Indeed after her mother's death in 1822 Lady Byron with Ada and her aged father Sir Ralph moved to various houses in Southern England. Her father died in 1825 and was buried at Kirkby Mallory. She never returned to live in Leicestershire. However, in contrast to her cousin Thomas she never tried to avoid her responsibilities to the locality and would make many visits to the area whenever circumstances demanded.

In 1824 Lady Byron had to appoint a curate for Kirkby Mallory and Earl Shilton and the man appointed was the Reverend John Longhurst. He was born on 12th. May 1800, gained his M.A. from Cambridge University and was then ordained by the Bishop of Lincoln. His first appointment was to the Leicestershire parishes of Knaptoft with Mowsley and Shearsby in 1823. For a young man of twenty four his appointment to Kirkby Mallory with Earl Shilton was to call for special qualities - and he would have no Rector to support him. On his first visit to Earl Shilton in 1824 he would have noticed a large new Independent Chapel being built and a Baptist Chapel in existence not more than 100 yards from the parish church which by this time was greatly in need of repairs and improvements. The population of Earl Shilton was around 2000 and that of Kirkby Mallory around 250 at this time. The principal occupation was frame-work knitting with all the frames being in the houses of the knitters. Conditions for the knitters were appalling, based on reports handed down in the locality and from evidence supplied some years later to a Royal Commission set up to look into the problems of the industry. Low prices, high frame rents, the trucking system, and various trade slumps were the main causes of these conditions. The rise of the Luddites had taken place only a few years earlier but the knitters were still being exploited by their masters.

Some idea of the state of affairs which existed can be understood from the following extract from *The Cradle and Home of the Hosiery Trade* published in 1940 by A.J.Pickering to celebrate the tercentenary of the first stocking frame into Hinckley in 1640 by William Iliffe:

> In June 1824 the stockingers ceased labour in order to obtain the rates prevailing in the year 1817. Failing to obtain their demands they carted their frames to the hosiers' warehouses without any consideration of the damage caused by their hasty removal. With no funds at their disposal they were eventually persuaded to return to work and agreed to again take in their frames. They appeared at the Parish Church on the following Sunday, with careworn countenances, tattered clothes and haggered looks. The prayers being concluded the worthy Vicar commenced his sermon, but was so overcome by the

picture of want and wretchedness before him that he was unable to proceed. He then gave vent to his feelings and said, so far as his example could avail, his efforts should be exerted on their behalf. He contributed generously and importuned others to do the same.

The situation at Earl Shilton would not have been any better than this appalling account from neighbouring Hinckley. Indeed the severe problems of the trade throughout the village would continue during Longhurst's appointment and beyond. There is much evidence handed down, confirmed by Longhurst, that the situation was much worse at Earl Shilton partly due to the lack of pastoral care in the village and the rebellious nature of the inhabitants. The population was growing rapidly without leadership and out of control.

To what extent Longhurst involved himself directly in village matters and the everyday lives of his parishioners is hard to discover, but there is no doubt that he quickly set about trying to improve the facilities at the church itself. There is a pamphlet dated 1850 preserved in the *Lovelace Byron Papers* which he had printed to become what we would now call his curriculum vitae (c.v.) and this includes the following extract:

He established the Sunday Schools in both Parishes (Kirkby Mallory and Earl Shilton) and notwithstanding the great poverty of the inhabitants at the Chapelry (Earl Shilton), chiefly poor framework knitters, he succeeded in erecting a commodious gallery for the accomodation of 180 children. The most valuable charitable institutions now existing at the Chapelry had their origins in Mr. Longhurst's exertions which the parishioners have kindly reciprocated by lasting tokens of their gratitude.

There is likewise a further interesting document discovered by Mr. Joe Lawrance, a churchwarden at Earl Shilton from 1966 to 1991, which records the presentation of a silver salver in 1840 to Longhurst from 'The inhabitants of the Chapelry of Earl Shilton' providing some useful information on conditions in the parish and Longhurst's appraisal of the situation. Here is an extract relating to Longhurst's alterations to the church.

My parishioners have suggested that I should here gratefully record the very essential service rendered to the honour of our common cause by those benefactors to whom I have been so deeply indebted: and before all, the liberality and life-giving assistance which I received from the noble family at Gopsall

Kirkby Mallory Hall

claim a lasting remembrance. At my first attempt to found the above school in 1825, encompassed with peculiar and almost insurmountable difficulties, Lord Howe wrote to me as follows:- 'I rejoice to hear of the formation of a Sunday School at Kirkby and though I have no connection whatever with Earl Shilton, yet I have the system of youthful education so much at heart, that I beg your acceptance of £6 from myself and £4 from Lady Howe towards the expenses of the first establishment of your school in that Parish'. His Lordship likewise gave me £10 towards the gallery mentioned hereafter, besides many smaller donations subsequently received for other benevolent uses at Earl Shilton. Lady Noel Byron gave £20 towards the said gallery, and is an annual subscriber to two charitable institutions more recently devised for the relief of the sick and necessitous.

It is revealing that the silver salver was inscribed from the 'inhabitants' rather than the 'parishioners' which might indicate that Longhurst took an interest in the affairs of the village in addition to his responsibilities to the church. It also gives the impression that Longhurst was keen to have the patronage of Earl Howe as he was the most influential person residing in this part of Leicestershire, because he knew it would be more difficult to court favour with Lady Byron. If things should not work out at Kirkby this contact would help him in his career.

CHAPTER FOUR

The Rev. John Longhurst and Mr. Charles Noel 1825-53

A major contributor to Longhurst's project was a Mr. Burley Scott of Carlton, Nottinghamshire who gave by his Will £100 towards maintaining the Church Sunday School. Mr Scott died on 29th. December 1843 and it appears that the money was invested for the purpose of building a separate Sunday School next to the Church and an article in the *Leicester Journal* towards the end of Longhurst's period added that it was 'hoped that the new incumbent will co-operate'.

Lady Byron talked at length with Longhurst about the difficult situation which faced him at Earl Shilton. No doubt he enjoyed the luxury of living at Kirkby Mallory rectory, a beautiful house built for the youngest sons of the Noel family. He would have enjoyed all the prestige of a Rector but without all the financial benefits. It would appear from a letter written by him which is in the *Lovelace Byron Papers*, that he received a stipend of £90 per annum from the proceeds of the Rectory.

In addition an amount of £10 per annum was to be paid to the Vicar or Curate to celebrate divine services and preach in the Chapel of Earl Shilton as an augmentation to the Vicar or Curate's revenue. This money came out of a farm in Congerstone through a bequest in the will of Verney Noel in the reign of Charles II. Whether Lady Byron made any other payment to Longhurst is not known.

Lady Byron probably did not bother Longhurst too much. Her main dealings with her Kirkby Mallory estates during this period would have been with her Land Agent, Charles Noel, the third son of the Rev. Thomas Noel, the absentee Rector. Charles was born in 1805 and in contrast to his father, enjoyed an excellent relationship with Lady Byron. It was through Charles that she was able to put into effect her many charitable projects in this area. It must be appreciated that her influence in this part of Leicestershire was enormous. *White's Directory* records Kirkby Mallory as having a population of 259 in 1846 and that Lady Byron owned all the soil, except for one farm owned by Thomas Jee. At this time the Directory shows the population of Earl Shilton as 2,220 adding 'The miserable condition of the poor framework knitters is somewhat alleviated by the occupation of fifty acres of land in spade husbandry let by Mr. Charles Noel at moderate rents as Lady Byron's Agent.'. The Directory goes on to say 'Lady Byron has built and supports two free schools (at Kirkby Mallory) for boys and girls. In addition to reading, writing and arithmetic, the boys to the number of about 100 are taught gardening chemistry, and each has a small plot of ground under his own cultivation.'

It is known that Lady Byron through her own initiative financed many schools in this part of Leicestershire as far apart as Fleckney and Market Bosworth. She certainly had a school at Earl Shilton and at least two samplers survive as evidence of this. The first one I discovered was done by Emma Brown, aged 10, in 1850 and belonged to Mr. Tom Dilks, a local headmaster. Emma Brown was his wife's grandmother. The second was done by Evelena Rowley Foster in 1851 and is displayed in Wygstons House Museum in Leicester. The museum's records state that she worked the sampler in cross-stitch with silk thread. Subsequently I have discovered further details of the school in Lady Byron's papers which appear later in the book.

As we have seen earlier Lady Byron was first cousin to Lord Melbourne, Queen Victoria's first Prime Minister. His wife Lady Caroline Lamb died in 1828 well before Melbourne's years as Prime Minister from 1835 to 1841. Lady Byron did not feel at ease in upper class society and avoided it as much as possible, preferring to become involved with schools, hospitals, reformatories, industrial schemes and projects like the Co-operative movement which would benefit the under privileged. It was in 1844 that the Co-operative movement first became established in Rochdale. She did, however, present her daughter Ada to London society, who at the age of nineteen, married a Lord King. Soon after the wedding and while Lord Melbourne was still Prime Minister, Lord King was created 1st. Earl of Lovelace. Ada therefore became his Countess outranking her mother in the social hierarchy. Byron himself had always been proud and yet annoyed with his rank as Baron which is the lowest in the peerage.

Peckleton House

Charles Noel lived at Peckleton House on the boundary of Kirkby Mallory and Peckleton. The house belonged to Lady Byron's estate and still exists as a home to this day. He appears to have had such a good relationship with Lady Byron that his absentee father all but disowned him. Charles had three brothers and at least one sister. They too enjoyed Lady Byron's friendship although they did not continue to live in Leicestershire. It must be said once again what a great pity it was that the Rev. Thomas Noel could not have accepted the situation which came about after his father's death. There is little doubt that this area of Leicestershire with an active and influential Rector would have benefited enormously. If the substantial parish of Earl Shilton could have received the benefit of a full time active curate it would not have been so neglected and impoverished. It is sometimes difficult for outsiders to appreciate this situation, and fully understand the harrowing accounts handed down in the village of the conditions the people then had to endure. The saying 'As poor as a stockinger' was very apt. Lady Byron and the local dignitaries such as Earl Howe of Gopsall Hall did much to alleviate this distress.

A search through the records of marriages at Earl Shilton Church shows that very few marriage ceremonies took place there at this time, although many couples from the village would have been married at Kirkby Mallory. However, what did happen according to old residents in the village emphasises the distress. To arrange a marriage cost time and money. To have the ceremony done at Earl Shilton by Longhurst would, no doubt, have cost more and been out of the question for the average couple, hence the very few marriages recorded.

The practice was for Earl Shilton couples wishing to marry to set off to walk to Kirkby Mallory. Once they had crossed the brook separating the parishes they would spend time around the fields and woods. When they returned to the village later in the day they would announce that they were now married! Of the copies of the marriage certificates which do exist for the period it is very noticeable how many persons just made a mark 'X' indicating that they could not even sign their own name.

One of the marriages which did take place at Earl Shilton was between William Swinney and Elizabeth Taylor on 30th. October 1815 performed by the Rev. Henry Pemble. This is mentioned not to pass comment on the bride's name, but to say that William Swinney was appointed Clerk and Sexton in 1850 to Earl Shilton Church and he also ran the village 'ragged' school. As this date coincides with the date of the Emma Brown sampler mentioned earlier there is a possibility that the Lady Byron school and the 'ragged' school were both financed by Lady Byron. William Swinney's son followed him as clerk and sexton in Earl Shilton and from 1898 until 1927 these duties were performed by his grandson Mr. W.S.Worthy.

Many examples of Lady Byron's care and consideration for this community exist and no doubt many have gone unrecorded. Many years ago the writer saw an old parish book which showed regular contributions from her. She also contributed to a Female Club in the village, and often referred to individuals in receipt of benefit, for example 'I do not like the idea of lessening Pegg's means of subsistence now that he is old and infirm.' And another 'I am happy that you see your way about the Shilton poor, and you may be assured the funds shall not be wanting to render the experiment effectual and permanent. I would give up half my own dinner rather than fail to help my fellow creatures at this crisis. Pray express my sentiments strongly on this point at the meeting as it may stimulate others. The great thing is not to delay as the people are starving.'

A very moving letter dated 13th. November 1846 also contained in the *Lovelace Byron Papers* best sums up Lady Byron's care and consideration.

> To the Honorable Lady Byron
> My Lady
>
> Knowing your sympathy and kindness I beg to lay my case before you fully believing that it is not your Ladyship's wish that the widow and children should be neglected and brought into trouble through being kept out of their right.
>
> When my late husband died he left a piece of ground to be sold to pay off a mortgage that was on it with the interest and all his lawful debts, the remainder of which I was put out to interest for the children and as I was sole executrix I expected to be allowed to put it out myself.
>
> In April I sold the ground to Mr. Noel for your Ladyship's use and up to the present time have not been able to get it settled nor have I yet received the deposit money. I think I may say I have been appointed to meet the lawyers 20 times and as often been disappointed.
>
> They say they will not pay the money unless I can find trustees to be found that the children receive the money when they come of age and it is wanted now to pay the debts with me. Your Ladyship these delays are very hurtful, I have seven children and my creditors are very urgent. I therefore bring my case before you knowing that a command from your Ladyship will be effectual. I beg to subscribe myself
> Your humble servant
> Mary Anne (Faulkes) ?
> An answer will be esteemed a great favor.

This letter calls for several comments. I cannot be sure of the surname of the lady in question as I cannot fully decipher the signature. It is quite likely that the lady received help to draft this letter. It is interesting to note the spelling used for words like 'favor' and 'Honorable'. It is likely that communications had already taken place with Charles Noel and he had suggested that she write a personal letter to Lady Byron. As the letter does not have the address of Lady Byron it is again likely that this letter was handed to

Charles Noel who forwarded it with his regular communications.

To some it may seem surprising that back in 1846 a member of what was often referred to as the 'labouring classes' could bypass all middlemen and cut through the red tape in such a manner, but this way of doing things was certainly not discouraged by Lady Byron. Taking an extract from one of Lady Byron's addresses to her tenantry reported in the *Leicester Journal* she states her instructions to Charles Noel on his becoming her agent as follows,

> *whenever there may be a difference of interest between a tenant and myself, I wish you to advocate the rights of the tenant as if they were your own. I can also testify that if any case which concerned the welfare of those dependent upon me, I appeared to him remiss, he represented the truth unsparingly towards me.*

Lady Byron's reply to the Earl Shilton lady was not copied but at the foot of the lady's letter in Lady Byron's handwriting are the words 'I replied that the money was paid.' It seems that this story had a happy ending.

It is understandable that Lady Byron from the facts so far illustrated was keen on the provision of schools for the working-class boys and girls including the rehabilitation of juvenile offenders. It was not only in Leicestershire that these were provided through her charitable works. She travelled around this country, sometimes taking Ada with her, and on the continent where she studied the system set up by Pestalozzi. She much preferred this type of education than the public school system through which of course Byron himself had passed. It must be emphasised again that Lady Byron took a personal interest in these schemes and took great care to see that they were managed properly. This has sometimes drawn criticism from biographers of Byron who have branded her uncaring and worse when she had to reprimand or dispense with the services of some manager of one of her projects. It must be remembered that in those days, when there was very little state regulation, some one had to make difficult decisions of this nature. Such criticism is hardly justified and the testimony of her tenants and others who benefited from her actions would certainly bear this out. It seems that Lady Byron's first consideration was always the 'working classes'. If she thought a manager did not adhere to this principle then she would take action.

Lady Byron continued with her other charitable interests. She helped and encouraged Elizabeth Blackwell an American who was to be credited with the honour of becoming the first woman doctor. When she first came to England, Lady Byron invited her to her home and helped her gain a position at St.

Bartholomew's Hospital. Lady Byron knew Florence Nightingale and her family and Dr. Blackwell remained on friendly terms with them both. Lady Byron kept up her interest in the anti-slavery movement and became a great friend of Harriet Beecher Stowe who was also a friend of Dr. Blackwell. Subsequently, after Lady Byron's death, when she had been attacked over her conduct towards her husband, it was Mrs.Stowe who wrote in her defence. It should be noted that, although living in the south of England, Lady Byron continued to support the Leicester Royal Infirmary. The infirmary records report her contributions as 'one of the largest'.

Despite these active interests Lady Byron herself did not enjoy the best of health. Her daughter Ada was similarly never particularly strong and was always subject to a breakdown in her health. Ada had three children, born in 1836, 1837 and 1839, the eldest named Byron with the title of Viscount Ockham, Anne Isabella after her grandmother; and Ralph. Lady Byron had a considerable influence on their upbringing.

The eldest, Byron, died in his mid-twenties, after running away to sea and appearing to reject his station in life, but was traced and returned to England. Lady Byron then placed him at Kirkby with Charles Noel for a time probably in order to satisfy his need for an outdoor, manual type of life. Ralph the youngest son was to live with his grandmother and was chiefly responsible for the collection of documents and letters we now know as the *Lovelace Byron Papers*. Ralph became the 2nd. Earl of Lovelace on his father's death and following the death of his first wife, married Mary Caroline Stuart Wortley. She, as Lady Lovelace, was to live until 1941 and frequently came to this area in connection with her estates. The daughter, Anne, was a very talented woman and particularly a great traveller who was one of the first English women to travel to Arabia. She had a great interest in Arab horses setting up the famous Crabbet Stud together with her husband, the writer Wilfrid Scawen Blunt.

Another letter to Charles Noel dated March 11th. 1846 gives further information of Lady Byron's charitable involvements.

Dear Sir,

Parker of Earl Shilton has a small piece of land to dispose of. I understand it joins some of Lady Byron's land and I thought if you were made acquainted with the distressed situation of the poor man and his wife you would interest yourself in their favor. I am told the purchase of this land would give a direct road to the Leicester turnpike from her Ladyship's farm which of course is desirable and which would induce her Ladyship to give more for it than any other person. The known kindness and generosity of her Ladyship has induced me thus to write to you as I believe the poor people are half lost, you will much oblige me by as early an answer as may suit your convenience- with kind regards to Mrs. Noel and yourself

> *I am dear Sir*
> *Yours respectfully*
> *Mary Bray*
> *New Buildings Hinckley*

Parker tells me there is nearly 3 acres of land.

Lady Byron, in addition to being well known in the neighbourhood, was of course a celebrity as the widow of the famous poet. We see this in a letter written by a Susanna Scudamore, a former tenant, who wrote to Charles Noel in 1849 requesting Lord and Lady Byron's autographs for a friend. Whether or not the request was granted is not known but it does demonstrate the continuing interest in the Byron saga.

Charles Noel was active in the temperance movement and it is quite likely, therefore, that he would have known Thomas Cook and possibly even have been one of the 500 or so passengers who went on that first historic railway excursion from Leicester to Loughborough in 1841 to a temperance meeting organised by Cook. He appears to have attended The Great Meeting Unitarian Chapel in Hinckley where a tablet was placed in his memory after his death. Lady Byron seems to have been happy to embrace most forms of Christian worship if she found it suited her circumstances being on friendly terms with people of a number of different denominations and with many clergymen. The lot of the poor stockingers of Earl Shilton showed no improvement and it is appropriate here to quote again from the text of Longhurst's response to the presentation of the silver salver by the inhabitants of Earl Shilton in 1840.

> *The solemn ordinances of the Church were either grossly neglected or rendered incapable of administering to godly edifying by mistaken notions of their intended good uses, and the consequent introduction of practices (particularly in the mournful solemnities of interring the dead) which were more befitting the benighted regions of Paganism and Idolatry than a land of Christendom.*

Longhurst continues:
My situation itself presented every discouragement. The Chapelry of your

Parish, subject to Kirkby, was then, and still continues, to the reproach of the Church, an anomaly in the County. A population of 2000 souls, without a resident clergyman, is a melancholy reflection - calculated to place the best interests of the Establishment in fearful jeopardy inasmuch as it curtails her accustomed ordinances, cripples her energies, lowers the standard of her excellence in the public credit, and weakens the attachment of her members by depriving them of the full amount of instruction edification and comfort to which they are pre-eminently entitled. This deficiency which has been a constant grief to my mind calls loudly for a remedy, and I have not failed to make it known in the most influential quarters, urging an alteration in your favour whenever an opportunity offers; and now that an Act of Parliament has recently been passed, giving power to effect such ecclesiastical changes, I see no impediment in the way of your accomplishing this most desirable object.

Quite what this act was intended to allow is not known but it did not have any immediate effect on the Earl Shilton situation. The absentee Rector and the parish in sequestration still blocked any progress:

Longhurst continues:

I found a church greviously neglected and unfrequented - but now I have the gratification of seeing the latter almost completely surrounded with new and substantial walls, while the former is usually filled by a devout and attentive audience.

Longhurst was making some impression on his troublesome parish and it is interesting to read his account of the youngsters of the parish, he continues:-

I also found the children of our Establishment entirely neglected and wandering about on the Lord's day - running in herds, like the swine in the Gospel, violently down the steep precipices of sin and folly. Ignorant of God and his Holy ways, their Sabbaths were chiefly employed in trespassing upon their neighbour, purloining or otherwise destroying their property, ruining themselves in body and soul by contracting in earliest youth the wretched habit of wallowing in the mire of vice, profaneness and immorality. But thanks to you, thanks to those noble benefactors who so liberally aided me in this and other benevolent schemes - thanks to the Almighty who put it into their hearts and yours so readily and cheerfully to co-operate with me, I can now point with paternal pride to the existence of an interesting and flourishing Sunday School, averaging from 160 to 180 children.

In 1843 a petition was presented to the House of Commons, signed by upwards of 25,000 Framework Knitters of the counties of Nottingham, Derby and Leicester to look into the 'severe privations' of the petitioners. This petition was accepted and the report was published in 1845. This report states

> The towns of Nottingham, Derby, Leicester, Hinckley, Loughborough, Belper, Earl Shilton, Thorpe, Kibworth, Barlestone, Whitwick, Sheepshead, Ruddington, Kimberley, Mansfield, Arnold, Sutton in Ashfield, Hucknall Torkard, Bulwell, Bridgeford, Heanor and Alfreton, formed respectively centres of inquiry.

The persons interviewed when the Commissioner visited Earl Shilton were John Walker, Isaac Abbott, Samuel King, Thomas Faulks, Joseph Taylor, Thomas Hopkins and Job Whitmore all framework knitters; Richard Wileman, James Pawley, William Spencer, William Cooper, Thomas Wileman, John Homer, John Hancock and Samuel Whiteman all manufacturers; Mr Randon, a baker; William Walker, a schoolmaster; and the Rev. John Longhurst. Just a few extracts will suffice here to help comprehend the situation:

Commissioner to Job Whitmore -
How many have you in family? Six in family with me.
At what age do your children commence seaming? Some they will put to it at four, or four and a half and five years. We are obliged to put them to it as soon as they can hold a needle in their hand. I was obliged to put one of mine to it under five years of age.
Do these young children work long hours at the seaming? Oh yes, from seven o'clock in the morning till 11 or 12 o'clock at night in the wintertime, many of them till they fall asleep upon the stool or chair they are sitting on. We can get nothing to nourish them before we put them to bed, they are almost starved in bedding.

Commissioner to William Walker -
Are there no free schools - no day schools? No.
Nor any infant schools besides? No.
Do you know what number of Sunday Schools there are? Four. One in connexion with the Church, one in connexion with the Independents, one in connexion with the Wesleyans, and one in connexion with the Baptists. I am

not aware whether there is one at the Primitive Methodists.
Do you know the number of scholars in any of those schools? I think about 140 at the Church school, and perhaps 220 in the other three.
Of what school are you master? Of the Greencoat school Alderman Newton's.
Do you receive any private pupils? Yes, I do.
What is the present number of the private pupils? About 25.
Are any of those children of framework knitters? No, none of them.
Is there a large class of boys who are running about totally uneducated? I should fancy, a very great many.
Do you know much of the condition of the dwelling houses of the poor people? They are some of them very bad indeed, destitute of all comforts, with no conveniences to them, and disgraceful and disgusting beyond all comparison.
Do you consider that there is a lamentable deficiency of education in the town? I do, very great.

The Commissioner put twenty six questions to Longhurst to which he gave very graphic replies. Here are some extracts:

What do you find to be the general moral condition of the people of the parish? I think, with regard to their dwellings, they are in a most offensive state. I wonder that there is the slightest sense of decency or moral feeling left among the females. It is shocking to see how they live, and the state in which they lodge. All the manufacturing girls are married in the family-way; they never think of coming to be married till they are close to confinement. I am sometimes in trepidation lest they should be taken ill whilst I am marrying them at the altar. They all intermarry; the whole parish are connected in that way, and it will frequently be the case that they have had a child or two before they come.
Many of these young women, I suppose are working in the frames? Yes, all framework knitters.
And do they lodge frequently together? Yes, young people, girls and boys, sleeping in the same rooms, and in the same beds, no doubt.
And do you attribute that to necessity, to the construction of the dwellings, or to what cause? Mainly to the construction of the dwellings, there not being a sufficient number of sleeping rooms, there being several beds in the same room, and the principle room being obliged to be adapted to the frames as a workshop. Many of the houses are in such a state of filth, where they are lost to all sense of decency, that you cannot positively go into some of them. The courtyards, in summer seasons where the filth is emptied into them, the noisome stench is so

> great you cannot possibly enter the court of a hot summer's day. Some years ago, when I first came here, I have been so affected by it as to be obliged to go to a neighbour's to get something to keep off sickness.
>
> Was not one of the friendly societies in this town recently a considerable loser by the failure of a hosier? They lost their all. I believe it was the richest friendly society in the place.
>
> You have no resident gentry here? Not one in the parish, everything devolves upon me - every public charity, and everything.
>
> It has been stated here that the framework knitters are unable, in many instances, to attend places of worship from want of clothing. Do you believe that to be a correct statement? I do. I have found cases where they have scarcely anything to cover over them. If they get up they have nothing to put on; dying for want of clothes to put on; and in some cases, I am afraid, a great deal attributable to want of care, and slatterness; the husband drinking or spending his time in idleness, and spending all he gets, and the wife pining for want of clothing and food; that is too much the case among them. There are a great many cases, I believe, where they cannot help it, where they are burdened with large families and low wages. I do not think, in such cases, they could provide themselves with clothes, so as to appear decent at a place of worship.

In all there are twenty seven pages of questions and answers relating to the Commissioner's visit to Earl Shilton. Perhaps this report was seen by Lady Byron or the contents made known to her because it was at about this time that she opened her school here.

Efforts were, however, now being made to educate adults and children. A Mechanics Institute was formed at Hinckley with this in mind and Charles Noel is shown as the Vice President. Children who attended school were allowed to bring work with them otherwise they would simply have been kept at home.

It appears that Earl Shilton being a manor held by the crown had an unusual privilege of choosing the equivalent of a 'Lord of the Manor' who held the Manor as a lessee of the Queen. A deed dated 1849 in the *Lovelace Byron Papers* shows that Lady Byron was awarded this privilege in that year. Meanwhile the Rev. Thomas Noel had surfaced again in 1847. A friend of Longhurst had written to him to say that he had seen the absentee Rector in Plymouth walking out with his young wife Henrietta and their young children and that he looked no more than 60 (He was in fact 72). His first wife Catherine had died some years before. Apparently this second marriage had brought him renewed vigour which provoked Longhurst to write to Lady Byron that 'there is no prospect of the demise of the Rector of this Parish, perhaps for years to come.' Longhurst then proceeds in the letter to complain again about his duties at Earl Shilton 'that unwieldy Chapelry of 2300 souls.'

One really does wonder why Longhurst put up with the situation over which he was always complaining. He had acquired numerous testimonials from influential persons as to his qualities and suitability and from a letter written by Earl Howe from Gopsall he appears to have made an attempt to find a new position

Gopsall, September 11th. 1842

My Dear Sir,

If my testimony of your fitness for the care of a more important Parish can be of the least service you are most welcome to it and it gives me much satisfaction to add my humble tribute to your merits as a zealous active Clergyman, whilst presiding over a poor, distressed population. I am confident you are well qualified for the permanent situation you desire and would well perform the duties of a Parish Minister; most sincerely do I trust you may succeed. With every kind wish etc. believe me

Very faithfully yours

Howe

Earl Shilton Church 1790

In spite of this rather restrained recommendation Longhurst did not get a new parish and it would appear likely that perhaps he was lacking in certain qualities. Another factor which seems rather strange is that in 1840 he purchased the 'Perpetual Advowson' of Dunton Bassett which is in effect the right to appoint the minister of that parish in perpetuity. The records show that he appointed his Uncle as Vicar and the Parish then passed to 'an influential dissenter'. Why did he not take the position himself at this time? We shall never know now, but something kept him at Kirkby and Earl Shilton which must have compensated for his many troubles. Many years later he did become Vicar of Dunton Bassett.

CHAPTER FIVE

The Rev. Frederick William Robertson

The 1850's transformation of Earl Shilton was largely influenced by certain events taking place in Brighton, Sussex. In 1847 the Rev. F.W.Robertson had been appointed Minister of Trinity Chapel Brighton and was to remain there until his death in 1853 at the early age of 37 years. During this time at Brighton he became one of the most well-known clergymen of his day. As well as endearing himself to his parishioners, particularly to the artisans and poor people, his preaching drew great attention. His sermons were published and distributed throughout the country and particularly in the U.S.A. He did not however set out to make the church his career, his first wish was for a military life. His father, grandfather and brothers had all distinguished themselves in this field, but after encouragement from others supported by his father he decided to enter the Church. He was a brilliant scholar who went to Oxford University in 1837 where he read widely and we are told that he made it his business everyday to commit to memory a part of the New Testament and eventually he could recite the New Testament in its entirety not only in English but also in Greek. He was at Oxford at the time of such men as Newman and Pusey but he was not inclined to become involved in any particular movement.

Robertson was fluent in several languages and well versed in literature, particularly Shakespeare, Wordsworth and Byron himself. He was ordained by the Bishop of Winchester on Sunday 12th July 1840. After spells at Winchester and Cheltenham, during which time he married, he was offered and accepted the parish of St. Ebbe's, Oxford in 1847. This was not a fashionable Oxford parish in the 'dreaming spires' tradition but a very poor and deprived one, however it was here that Robertson was to display his talents. He quickly won the confidence of the parishioners and, like Newman earlier, attracted a substantial number of undergraduates to his services. Remarkably though, after only two months at St. Ebbe's an offer was made for him to become Minister at Trinity Chapel, Brighton.

Quite what the reason was for this sudden appointment after so short a time we are not sure. Robertson at first declined to accept in the genuine belief that it would be betraying the people of the parish of St. Ebbe's. However the Bishop of Oxford, when the matter was referred to him, suggested that Robertson should accept. His stand on what he considered the truth had during his time at Winchester caused him to disagree with the Bishop before his appointment to the Bishopric but this does not seem to have played any part. The Bishop in question was Samuel Wilberforce, a son of William Wilberforce the anti-slavery campaigner, who was years later to clash with Charles Darwin over his book *The Origin of Species*. Robertson's health was causing some concern probably because of the punishing schedule he set himself.

Taking the Bishop's advice Robertson duly accepted the office of Perpetual Curate of Trinity Chapel, Brighton. This period between August 1847 to his death in August 1853 was to see his rise to fame, not only through his preaching but also because of his determination to pursue an independent line of thought when the clergy were expected to belong to a particular faction, and use their influence accordingly. This, together with his support of the working classes and the poor, caused him to be attacked by many as being a 'Socialist'. One of his chief desires was to bridge the gap between the wealthier and poorer classes and this he did by supporting the education of the latter in every way possible.

Robertson's enormous energy and knowledge were such that his lectures and sermons would be quite lengthy and academic by modern standards, including those given to persons who had only received a very basic education. Lectures on poetry for instance and on the burning issues of the day would be delivered with great detail and passion. Even if it often went over the heads of some of his audience he at least caused them to think hard and aspire to greater things.

Because of his independent thought he was often challenged on certain issues to express his views which would then bring praise and condemnation alike. He was often accused of bringing politics into the Church. Some examples of this are given below.

In 1849 a famous clairvoyant came to Brighton, Robertson was invited to his seances which he at first refused but afterwards attended. It was found that in Robertson's presence there were no revelations, the clairvoyant blaming Robertson's presence for this.

He pronounced on such topical matters as Women's rights, Early closing for Shops, Sunday Postal Deliveries and Keeping the Sabbath in general. A particular reason for debate on the latter subject was caused by the intention to open the 1851 Great Exhibition at the Crystal Palace on a Sunday. A petition was signed by all the clergymen of the area against this, but Robertson firmly refused to sign partly on the grounds that it would enable the working classes to visit, and nobody ever complained at the activities of the upper classes on a Sunday. It should be said that Robertson firmly believed in Sunday as a special day but he took a common-sense approach to the matter.

When elections took place at Brighton in 1852, Robertson voted not out of duty or as was expected of him, but on the issues of the day. Voting in those days was not by secret ballot, and all present knew for whom he was casting his vote. When his vote went for a particular candidate the crowd cheered loudly particularly as all the other clergy had voted for the other side!

Soon after his arrival in Brighton, Robertson was introduced to Lady Byron who had a house in the area. They immediately became friends and discussed matters of common interest. It was intended that Robertson would become her literary executor after her death and perhaps publish her views on her relationship with Byron and the separation. As with many other plans of the unfortunate Lady Byron, this was frustrated by Robertson's early death which affected her greatly.

During the first few months of 1853 Robertson had become very ill indeed. Not only had his physical condition deteriorated but his mental powers and his thought process were affected, but this only forced him to greater effort to overcome his difficulties. Severe head pains became unbearable at times and finally on 4th April 1853 he collapsed in West Street, Brighton. Robertson still continued with his duties, but after consulting his doctor he was persuaded to take a short holiday in Cheltenham. The respite was brief and on his return to Brighton his condition worsened.

By now all his many friends and parishioners realised that something had to be done and they got together to raise money for him to appoint an assistant. It has to be remembered that Robertson was taking services up to three times on a Sunday often to a packed Church. Preparation work must have been enormous. In addition he was writing and answering letters on a multitude of topics arising often from points he made in his own sermons. This was done on top of pastoral work which he regarded with the utmost importance. Clearly this would have been too much even for the fittest of men and he welcomed the offer of a curate which would enable him to share some of these duties. The man he selected for this position was the Rev. Ferdinand Ernest Tower who was previously Curate at a neighbouring parish, Hurstpierpoint.

Robertson wrote on 17th May 1853 -

Mr. Tower has accepted my Curacy and both his father and mother whose letters I have seen, are pleased. He is a gentleman thoroughly in earnest, hardworking and attached to me. Our spheres and powers lie in different directions, which will prevent the possibility of collision and as he will take the afternoon sermon I shall have leisure for more pastoral work, at the prospect of which I rejoice, for I cannot say how humiliated I feel at degenerating into the popular preacher of a fashionable watering place. In addition to this he has strong health, so that I shall not have compunction in delegating work to him when I am unfit for it.

At this time Robertson was 37 and Tower 32 and it seemed a partnership full of promise. Both came from military families, were well educated and very disciplined essentially with an upper middle class background, but were dedicated to giving a helping hand to the poor and deprived. Both were very keen to raise the standard of the working classes through education and this, when coupled with Robertson's increasing influence on church development and thinking through his sermons and lectures, seemed an ideal situation.

Unfortunately one item had been overlooked which one would have thought could have been taken for granted and that was the approval of the Vicar of Brighton, the Rev. H.M.Wagner. He had the right to veto or sanction any appointment. On learning of this proposal he was adamant that he would not accept Tower's nomination. The reason given by the Vicar was set out in correspondence between Robertson and the Vicar. It is brought together in a quite forceful letter from Robertson denouncing the conduct and the reasoning of the Rev.Wagner. This important letter is printed here in full below and the words speak for themselves. In addition to the letter to the Vicar, a printed circular exists in Lady Byron's personal papers together with a press cutting giving much of the same information as contained in the letter, but it is addressed to the committee responsible for supporting the appointment of the

The Rev. Frederick William Robertson

Curate. Those who had contributed to the fund were very upset and as a result there was much turmoil in the church affairs at Brighton.

> *60 Montpelier Road: June 22, 1853*
> REVEREND SIR, - *I have to acknowledge the receipt of your note of the 18th inst., in which you recommend me to present another nominee for your approval, and offer to find some one to supply his place till appointed. I regret that I cannot reciprocate the bland tone of this last communication; for I confess that patronising offers of favour seem to me out of place, when that which is asked for, and still peremptorily refused, is the redress of a wrong. And I regret to find that you view the matter between us, your own part in it in particular, in a much more light and easy way than that in which any one else will see it. Suffer me to be explicit; for the forbearance of my first letter having been unappreciated, I am compelled to speak English that cannot be misunderstood.*

I cannot offer another nominee; nor is it in my power to accept at your hands the favour of any aid such as you offer.

I will examine, first, the objection against Mr. Tower, and how far it is possible for me to pass smoothly by the rejection of my friend, and receive a favour from his rejector.

The charge, as I collect it from your words, assumes two shapes :-
1. Unbecoming behaviour in interfering with the affairs of the Lewes Deanery Branch of the Society for Promoting Christian Knowledge - a society established in your parish.
2. Unbecoming conduct towards yourself.

With respect to the first, it must be remembered that, though Brighton be the head-quarters of the Branch Society, and the Vicar of Brighton at present chairman, it is not a Brighton society, but one belonging to the whole Deanery of Lewes, and that, as a clergyman of the Deanery, and member of the Committee, Mr. Tower had an equal right with yourself to move any measure he thought right. It is as incorrect to imply that he interfered with a parochial society, or the prerogatives of the Vicar of Brighton, as it is unjust to insinuate that, as a curate, he took too much upon him. The country clergy gave him - he did not assume - a leading part in the discussion, because he was furnished with considerable information from the Parent Society.

2ndly. With respect to Mr. Tower's personal conduct to yourself. An overwhelming majority of the Committee - all, indeed, I believe, except those who are bound by some personal tie to yourself, and, therefore, perhaps naturally, feel with you - are prepared to assert that Mr. Tower's conduct on those occasions was that of a Christian and a gentleman. If necessary, I shall call for that testimony. I could call for more, but I have no wish for recrimination.

For the question is not, after all, whether Mr. Tower spoke warmly to you, or you to him, nor whether Mr. Tower was right or wrong in the course which he at least pursued conscientiously ; but the question is, whether that course was sufficient ground for permanent unforgivingness on your part, and whether such offences as a personal difference with yourself, and interference in a favourite society of your own, admitting them to have existed to their fullest extent, are just grounds for the rejection of one whom you yourself admit to be in conduct and doctrine an exemplary Christian minister. No bishop would exclude from his diocese on such grounds ; if he did, all England would ring with the news of the transaction.

I will now advert, with much regret, to your treatment of myself, which will account for my inability to adopt suddenly the suave tone of your last communication. I fix on a single instance.

On Trinity Sunday, during our first accidental interview between services, I told you several times that I was desirous of postponing the subject of the curacy till the morrow, and anxious to return home, as I had to prepare for the duties of the afternoon pulpit, and was much pressed for time. In spite of this, within half an hour you abruptly and unnecessarily invaded a privacy which you knew I had such anxious reasons to keep calm and sacred from interruption ; and with yourself you forced upon me as a witness a gentleman personally unknown to me. The witness system, in a conversation between gentleman, used by you to me even more offensively on a previous occasion, is in itself a very objectionable proceeding. It is scarcely necessary to say that the interruption incapacitated me from addressing my congregation on the intended subject.

I select this fact, not because it is the only instance, by many, of your discourtesy, but because your own witness was present. These are not supposed to be the manners of civilised society; nor can the grievance of them be obliterated by a few smooth lines, not of apology, but of patronage. It is curious to see with what marvellously different degrees of tenacity men retain the recollection of their own discourtesy to others, and that of others towards them. At the end of a couple of weeks, all that you said and did to me seems to have vanished from your mind ; at the end of two years, Mr. Tower's so-called transgression against yourself is as indelible as ever.

I much regret that it is my duty to write thus plainly, because I forsee that the publication of this letter may be necessary,- the right of doing which I reserve to myself ; more especially as your uncalled-for offer to supply my pulpit may give a fallacious aspect to the whole affair, unless I very distinctly show what the question at issue is, and what it is not.

I can offer no other nominee, because I cannot admit your right of rejection on personal grounds. I am informed that you have a legal right ; but I believe the whole world will deny your moral right. I know that, as you have stated, you are irresponsible by law, and can reject without assigning a reason. But irresponsibility is one thing in despotic Russia, and another thing in free England. No man can be irresponsible to public judgement in the exercise of a solemn public trust.

Nor can I subject another friend to the chance of your discovering, as in Mr. Macleane's case, a ground of objection in the circumstance of his taking pupils ; or, as in Mr. Tower's case, in the fact of his having had the misfortune *to vote against you an indefinite number of years ago. Lastly, I will not subject any gentleman again to the indignity of being asked for guarantees for conduct, or willingness to support, blindfold, the particular societies which you choose to name.*

I have the honour to be, Reverend Sir,
Your Obedient servant,
Fred. W. Robertson.

The vicar would not yield and rather than cause dissension in the locality and cause a rift in church affairs Robertson had no choice but to accept defeat. Heart broken and desperately ill, he tried to continue on alone, but just two weeks later on Sunday 5th. June he was to preach what was to be his last sermon in Trinity Chapel.

Robertson did not of course know it would be his final appearance at Trinity Chapel but the text for this sermon was taken from the thirteenth and final chapter of The Second Epistle of Paul the Apostle to the Corinthians verse eleven. "Finally, brethren, farewell. Be perfect, be of good comfort, be of one mind, live in peace; and the God of love and peace shall be with you."

Robertson now confined to his room for most of the time, was gradually becoming weaker although there were occasions when he thought he was again regaining his strength. He says in one of the few letters he wrote at this time that he went out for a short walk but found he could not walk back and that a tradesman unknown to him came out and offered him a seat in his shop and another poor man took his arm.

Intense suffering, excruciating pain and paralysis marked his last few days. The last words he wrote ended as follows - 'I think now that I shall not get over this. His will be done ! I write in torture !'

Among those who visited him in these last days was Lady Byron but it is not recorded how often he saw and conversed with Tower. On 15th. August he died, conscious almost to the end, in the early hours of the morning.

The funeral took place one week later on Monday 22nd. August 1853 and although it was intended to be private practically the whole of Brighton turned out in respect for the man they genuinely loved and respected. It is reported that every shop on the route of his funeral procession from his home in Montpelier Road to the Cemetery on the Lewes Road closed and that the pavements and balconies were crowded with sorrowing spectators. The town was in mourning and over two thousand persons pressed into the Cemetery. Among the mourners was Lady Byron who was devastated by his early death.

She stated that she would not use a carriage and that she was not fit even to walk behind the hearse. She stood in the cemetery next to a Mr. A.J.Ross a mutual friend. She told Ross that she 'could not but painfully discover that he was sowing himself beyond his strength and that his very calm was a hurricane.'

A monument was erected at his grave by the people of Brighton which still stands today not far from the entrance to the Cemetery. When I visited the grave in 1988 it was not long after the hurricane which hit the South of England at the end of the previous year and one could not help but notice a large tree which had crashed to the ground thankfully just missing his memorial. Perhaps then we can reflect on Lady Byron's words and add that the twentieth century hurricane was careful not to disturb this nineteenth century hurricane!

A fund was established to benefit Robertson's widow and two children to which Lady Byron contributed £300. Trinity Chapel though closed as a place of worship still stands at the bottom of Duke Street in Brighton close to 'The Lanes' with a plaque on the wall to the memory of Robertson.

The Reverend Ferdinand Ernest Tower

CHAPTER SIX

The Rev. F. E. Tower and the Earl Shilton Transition

A few months before the death of Robertson, Lady Byron had to endure a more personal bereavement, that of her daughter Ada, Countess of Lovelace on 27th. November 1852. Robertson had visited Lady Byron during the final months of Ada's illness and it is difficult to imagine the effect these two deaths had on her. There had been much concern and aggravation over Ada's activities prior to her final illness. She and her mother had been friendly for a number of years with Charles Babbage famous for his invention of a calculating machine and often referred to as the first computer. Both Ada and her mother were interested and skilled in mathematics. Ada was eager to work with Babbage on his systems, and their work in this field is acknowledged to this day. Unfortunately Ada became caught up in a system to bet on horse races and incurred heavy losses which Lady Byron had to deal with and which caused further alienation between her and both Ada's husband and Babbage. It is not difficult to imagine that Lady Byron had over the years since her marriage felt very let down by people she trusted and with the death of Robertson to whom she could relate she had lost her dearest friend. She did however have many female friends and the love of her three grandchildren.

The Earl Shilton situation was still one of her continuing concerns and at this distressing time she received a letter from the Rev. G.E.Bruxner and Isaac Hodgson Esq. at the request of the Leicestershire Church Extension Fund on this matter. From a report published in the *Leicester Journal* it states - 'From the Rev. J. Longhurst Curate of Earl Shilton for aid towards the maintenance of a temporary Curate in that parish. This application was refused in the first instance, the Committee being of the opinion that this case hardly came within the object of the fund. But their attention having been again called to the state of the parish a resolution was passed in September last (1852) requesting the Rev. G.E.Bruxner and Isaac Hodgson Esq. to communicate with Lady Byron the Patroness of Kirkby Mallory and Earl Shilton on the subject of a disunion of those parishes and a better provision for the pastoral care of the latter'

Bruxner was the Rector of nearby Thurlaston and a Justice of the Peace at Market Bosworth. He knew Lady Byron and probably served on the board of the Leicestershire Church Extension Fund. No record is available of a reply because soon after the report was published on April 2nd. 1853 matters would resolve themselves to some extent.

But first another look at Lady Byron's relationship with her tenants would be appropriate and the following is an extract from a report from the *Leicester Journal* in 1853:

> *Lady Byron's Rent Audit - On Monday last Charles Noel of Peckleton House held the rent audit of the Right Hon. Lady Byron at the Town Hall, Hinckley... where a good and substantial dinner was provided under the superintendance of Mr. Wm.Gent for her Ladyship's numerous tenantry of Elmesthorpe, Kirkby Mallory, Peckleton and other villages. After the cloth was drawn... a letter was read by Mr. Noel from her Ladyship in which she expressed the deep interest she felt in the welfare of her tenantry and intimated her desire at all times to meet their wishes and promote their happiness in every possible way. These benevolent expressions and desires on the part of her ladyship were received with hearty cheers...*
>
> *In the evening the wives, sons and daughters with friends were invited to tea in the Hall, which had been tastefully decorated for the occasion, after which the company enjoyed themselves with music, dancing and other recreations for the night and an excellent band being engaged for the occasion...*

The most notable feature of this report and the reason for including it here is to show that Lady Byron was much happier dealing with this type of relationship. This leads one to wonder if she would not have been better to live at Kirkby Mallory Hall which she still owned, rather than constantly moving from one property to another in the south of England. Her health would surely have been much better in the country.

It will be noted from the last chapter that Lady Byron was amongst those who attended Robertson's funeral in Brighton on Monday August 22nd. 1853. She was, however, unaware that on this very same day by a strange coincidence another death had taken place far away in Plymouth. The Rector of Kirkby Mallory with Earl Shilton and Elmesthorpe had died on that day aged 79, now leaving the way open for Lady Byron to deal with the situation of the parishes. Another person too would have learnt of the death of the Rev. Thomas Noel with eager anticipation and that was the Rev. John Longhurst the Curate of the above parishes. Having struggled on alone for around 30 years he had high hopes of promotion and at the age of 53 he could perhaps begin to enjoy the fruits of his labours. After all he probably would not have remained at Kirkby unless he had expectations of becoming its Rector one day.

What actually took place in the Brighton area after the rejection of Tower by the Vicar of Brighton we only know in relation to the sad death of Robertson. But from events that later followed we can be fairly certain that Lady Byron had met with Tower and indeed may have discussed the Kirkby Mallory and Earl Shilton situation with him. From Robertson's letter quoted earlier we know that he had communicated with Tower's parents on the subject of him coming to Trinity Chapel and we know that Tower had invited Robertson to Hurstpierpoint in 1851 and that they had conversed in that year on the question of Sunday Observance. The effect on Tower of the rejection must have been devastating to him and to his family, some of whom also held offices in the Church of England, and without Robertson there was nothing to keep him at Brighton. In any case there was much recrimination taking place in Brighton following the Vicar's veto and it must be added that some of this reached the ears of the dying Robertson, who anxious not to see a divided Church asked if he needed to intervene. To avoid further problems then Tower would have no objection to leaving the area.

We know that Lady Byron and Robertson were good friends, and had mutual respect, but we can ask how Tower fitted into the relationship. Tower was born on the 4th. October 1820 at Weald Hall, Essex, the family home of the Tower family since 1752. He was the fifth son of Christopher Thomas Tower and Harriet daughter of Sir Thomas Beauchamp Proctor Bart, who was M.P. for Harwich from 1832-7 and grandson of Christopher Tower and Elizabeth only daughter of George Baker of Elemore Hall, Co. Durham. This George Baker married Judith, a granddaughter of a Sir Mark Milbanke. Lady Byron's father Sir Ralph Milbanke was a great grandson of this same Sir Mark which meant that Lady Byron and the Rev. Tower were both descended from him, in other words they were distant cousins. What is even more important is that Lady Byron, as we have seen earlier, was born at Elemore Hall on Thursday 17th. May, 1792 which was then the home of George and Isabella

Baker who as well as being relations were also great friends of Lady Byron's parents. You will remember from the first chapter that Lady Byron was named Isabella after Mrs.Baker.

After the Milbankes had left the north-east to return to Kirkby, their beautiful house on the cliffs at Seaham was rented to the Bakers and after the separation Lady Byron paid a visit on her trip to the north. Particularly in those days family ties endured over many generations and Tower must, I feel, have been known by Lady Byron probably before Robertson became their mutual friend. One other relationship worth mentioning, is that Tower was a direct descendant through the Bakers of Sir Henry Firebrace of Stoke Golding, Leicestershire. Firebrace was Clerk-Comptroller of the household to Charles II and was the person principally concerned in attempting the delivery of King Charles I from his prison at Carisbrooke Castle which was to have been achieved by the King sawing through the bars of his window with a file. A marble monument to Sir Henry was erected in Stoke Golding Church.

Although it would not have been admitted at the time one can only feel that a possible cause of the Vicar of Brighton's intransigence was a fear of Trinity Chapel dominating the principal parish church. Robertson's fame was attracting considerable attention and he was preaching to large congregations, but not all his views would have met with the approval of a more conservative Vicar. The presence of another formidable young clergyman in partnership with Robertson was perhaps more than he could contemplate. He had now lost Robertson and was about to lose Tower.

The news of the death of the Rev. Thomas Noel would be with Lady Byron almost as she returned home from Robertson's funeral. She had many options open to her and she quickly got in touch with the Bishop of Peterborough, with the letter from Bruxner and Hodgson firmly in her mind. Three items needed her attention then:

(1) Division of the parishes of Earl Shilton and Elmesthorpe from Kirkby Mallory.
(2) A new Rector for Kirkby Mallory.
(3) A new Vicar for Earl Shilton who would also be Rector of Elmesthorpe.

First she needed assistance from the diocese of Peterborough and a note appears in the *Lovelace Byron Papers* as follows:

> Mr Henry Pearson Gates presents his respectful compts to Lady Noel Byron and informs her Ladyship that the patronage of the Perpetual Curacy of Earl Shilton is with her Ladyship without any limitations and it will be the Bishop's

duty to require the Incumbent thereof to build a house by mortgaging the Preferment under the provisions of the 1st. and 2nd. Vict. c. 106 and Mr. Henry Pearson Gates apprehends that a part of the Glebe may be made available for that purpose. The annexation of the Rectory of Elmesthorpe may be proceeded with before or after the admission of the new incumbent as may best suit Lady Byron's wishes.
Peterborough 23rd. September 1853

This letter sets in motion the first of these objectives and it is quite likely that Tower was assisting Lady Byron in these tasks. Longhurst wrote two letters to Lady Byron setting out what he believed should be done at both Kirkby Mallory and Earl Shilton and stating that should she feel a younger man was needed for the huge tasks which lay ahead his son was also available; but taking particular care to say that he was available for the vacant post. He took great delight in telling Lady Byron that some of the most important people in the parishes had stated that he was the man for the job and testimonials he had previously had printed for circulation were, he believed, ample evidence for this.

Lady Byron, however, had other ideas. She informed him that she was not appointing him either as Rector of Kirkby Mallory or as the new Vicar of Earl Shilton. The reason for not doing so cannot be stated for certain but there are indications. Longhurst had pestered Lady Byron over the Earl Shilton situation for years, and clearly he did not welcome his duties there, and he made his views known to many influential people. Lady Byron had been embarrassed over the situation but there was really only one course open to her and that was to pay for a curate herself. Longhurst was not going to pay for a permanent curate himself out of his funds, and there is no suggestion that the people of Kirkby Mallory and Earl Shilton were ready to do, as the people of Brighton had done for Robertson and provide finance to support a Curate. Certainly the Rev. Thomas Noel was not, as he seemed to relish the embarrassment he was causing Lady Byron, and he showed no concern for his parishioners. 'The demoralised state (of Earl Shilton) is unhappily irremedial till the minister there should attend his duties in a spirit more consistent with the principles of Christianity' stated Lady Byron. Finally, no financial support was forthcoming from the Diocese of Peterborough.

Lady Byron certainly knew that Longhurst had bought the living of Dunton Bassett and that he had unsuccessfully applied for at least one other parish as details appear in her private papers and this would have influenced her.

Anyway Lady Byron knew, at first hand, that if the problem at Earl Shilton was to be corrected then it needed a man of many qualities and of course she knew such a man. With the Rev. Thomas Noel gone she was prepared to take action to remedy the situation and for all time.

Longhurst was of course very hurt and annoyed at being passed over and sat down and wrote the following letter to Lady Byron. It is impossible for us to judge the situation with certainty but Lady Byron knew exactly what she wanted.

Kirkby Mallory
Hinckley
September 6th. 1853

My Lady,

Thanks for one ray of sympathy - we were prostrated by your first letter. The poor distressed mother of <u>thirteen</u> children born in the house with ten of these on hand did <u>nothing but weep</u> and having myself a severe attack of influenza it completely unfitted me for my morning duty at Earl Shilton on Sunday. However I was much gratified to announce to my flock the <u>intended change</u> which I have ever advocated as recorded in my private address of 1840.

Your Ladyship's judgement... may be right but appealing to a noble Christian Lady (in whose affliction I have most heartily sympathised) and of superior understanding and a very high order of intellect, I shall be excused for saying, it would indeed be far more dignified and graceful if tempered with reconciliation and mercy. Methinks it would be God like.

My case is not common, <u>it has no parallel</u> left alone for 30 years without a Rector to wage the battle with sin, the world and the devil at that unwieldy Chapelry of 2300 souls.

I have the testimony of Mr. Charles Noel that "nobody like myself can manage them" but it has been at <u>a fearful cost</u> called always in the roughest weather to bury their dead in that bleakest of Churchyards (not infrequently when confined to my room by cold taken in performing the same duty a day or two before) Now at the age of 53 <u>every tooth in my head has been extracted</u> save my two eye teeth, with this great infirmity as a reminder, still doing my usual duties when I need to be in a position, on any sudden emergency to fall back upon the aid of a Curate, I am turned out sold up and sent adrift like Samson shorn of my strength without a home, without a ?!(word illegible)

In 1826 you kindly said "I am aware of the difficulties which you represent as attached to your situation at Kirkby and wish if it were in my power to obtain more liberal conditions for you" but now the power is come the will is gone, though I have uniformly laboured to maintain my own principles and to do my duty without in any way interfering with the actual ground occupied by your Ladyship etc...

Believe me my Lady
Your Ladyship's ever faithful and obedient servant
John Longhurst

The letter reached Lady Byron next day. It prompted an immediate response and fortunately she did copy her reply for her own records. It should be noted that Lady Byron would only take a copy of one of her letters if she thought it important enough to make one.

Esher,
September 7th. 1853

Lady Byron's copy

I felt called upon by your letter yesterday to protest against the construction you put on my motives for not presenting you to the living at Kirkby Mallory.

My refusal had no connection whatever with circumstances personal to myself- my sole consideration is the welfare of the Parish - and if I should not judge wisely with respect to the future incumbent it will not be from the influence of private interest or feeling. The high testimonials to which you have referred afford me the relief of hoping that whatever may be your present difficulties you will not long remain without a place of souls.

With sincerely held wishes
Your obt. Servant
A.I.N.B.

It is noticeable that Lady Byron's reply only mentioned Kirkby Mallory. Perhaps Longhurst had made it known directly or through his actions that he did not want to become the new Vicar of Earl Shilton but we do not know. Perhaps he was hoping his son would be appointed. Either way the result was the same - no job!

A report in the *Leicestershire Mercury* dated 14th January, 1854 reads

The Rev. J. Longhurst M.A. having announced the probability of his removal from Kirkby Mallory, the parishioners and inhabitants of Earl Shilton united together and presented him with an elegant silver tea and coffee service, with inscriptions testifying the faithful discharge of his pastoral duties during a residence of 30 years. The Rev. W.R.Burgin delivered an address to Mr. Longhurst which was suitably responded to.

The *Leicester Journal*, however, reports that Longhurst preached at Kirkby Mallory Church at a Whitsuntide Service in 1857 to a large congregation so perhaps wounds were quickly healed. For many years after leaving Kirkby he was Vicar of Dunton Bassett a village about ten miles away, of which, as we have seen, he was also the Patron.

At this point it is necessary to reflect on the character and judgement of Lady Byron. With one or two notable exceptions she has been the subject of much criticism from biographers of Lord Byron for her attitude towards him in particular, and some have then gone on to use all their literary skills to denounce everything she did by interpreting her motives in the worst possible light. It should be remembered that Byron was a genius and all his thoughts and actions were played out in full on the world stage but a genius does not make an ideal companion. Byron was born to lead and not to follow and his restless mind affected just about everyone he came into contact with during his short life. He was, as Samuel Rogers described him, 'like a star that thro' the firmament shot and was lost in its eccentric course dazzling, perplexing.'

As the nineteenth century proceeded, writers were desperately keen to obtain statements from anyone, particularly ageing servants who had known the couple in those earlier days. Leading questions were asked and interviewers usually got the answers they were looking for. Many used the Byron contact however small to enhance their own importance.

Lady Byron as we have seen did not belong in this situation. She enjoyed poetry and the arts as a pastime and after first meeting Byron she probably succumbed to his charms in common with most of the young ladies of the day. Byron could not have lived the contented life of a country squire or man about town. He was destined to become a wanderer. Lady Byron may have adjusted to his life style but those few weeks away from him at Kirkby with her parents determined the future for her. Once in the hands of the lawyers there was no turning back and Lady Byron had to live the type of life she had now carved out for herself.

Byron spoke out for the oppressed in his speeches, writings and poetry, but Lady Byron, like most people, did not possess these talents but she certainly concentrated a lot of her efforts into giving direct help to the poor and needy. Perhaps in the end they both got what they deserved for Byron usually tired of his liaisons with women and Lady Byron spent the remainder of her life as a widow showing no further interest in matrimony.

Most writers on Byron tend to identify with him and not Lady Byron. However if you were of the poorer classes Lady Byron's practical assistance would have counted for far more than Byron's words at that time in Earl Shilton! Byron was a hero to the people of Greece, just as Lady Byron was to the less conspicuous population of Earl Shilton.

On the Longhurst question no doubt many of the celebrated Byron writers would have branded Lady Byron as ruthless, unfeeling, bitter intransigent etc. but they would have gone no further in their research. It would not have been their concern that a village of over 2000 people was completely lacking in pastoral care, that the terrible conditions of the inhabitants was causing so much concern, that the parish church was in a poor state of repair, and that charity was the only hope of most villagers. Lady Byron did not turn away from these troubles. She was faced with the choice which today leaders of industry are often confronted with – do you promote a faithful retainer to an important position requiring drive and initiative or do you appoint a dynamic highly qualified young manager who is conversant with modern thinking? She chose the latter.

The new Vicar of Earl Shilton was to be the Rev. F.E.Tower now thirty three years of age. Young, fit and very able to tackle the problems 'at that unwieldy Chapelry of 2300 souls' as Longhurst wrote, and in addition to play a full part in village life. It would be very different from working with Robertson at Brighton, and he set about his task immediately. So now number three of the objectives had been achieved and Tower confirms this in a short letter to Lady Byron from his family home.

Weald Hall
March 6th.1854

Dear Lady Byron,
I thank you many times for your plain liberal letter today which relieves me of some thoughts and gives a start to my parish proposal ahead of much difficulty. I have written by this post to my brother - in - law Mr. Henry Kingscote at present Secretary to the Government Cathedral Committee. I requested him to act as the required Trustee. You may hear again in a day or two.
Pray believe me most gratefully yours,
Ernest Tower.

On 9th. March he wrote again enclosing his brother- in-law's answer. There is also a letter in Lady Byron's private papers from the Rev. John

Fisher of Higham on the Hill agreeing to act as a Trustee. This letter is addressed to Lady Byron personally and would be an answer to a previous letter and request from Lady Byron. John Fisher would have been from the same family as Geoffrey Fisher, the former Archbishop of Canterbury, possibly his grandfather. Lady Byron was now communicating with Charles Noel on almost a daily basis. On 2nd. October she writes,

As it is my wish to ensure the value of the Perpetual Curacy of Earl Shilton, I can do so... by adding to the Glebe. Pray inform me what land I have in that Parish or contiguous in Elmesthorpe which might be appropriated.'

However, she was frustrated in this plan to help when she was informed by her legal advisor as follows,

Dr. Lushington has put me right about the law which Mr. Wharton had mistaken, as land cannot be attached to Glebe out of an entailed estate. I must therefore make another arrangement and not wishing to lay down a sum of ready money I must make some other arrangement for the payment during my life.

She did however have to resort to giving a sum of money as will be seen later. She wrote again to Charles Noel,

I directed Mr. Tower how to find your house. Let Mr. Tower see all the old church at Elmesthorpe and explain to him how few inhabitants there are in that parish. He should also look at different spots where a parsonage might be erected.

And interestingly

give him proofs of the better disposition of the manufacturing population - so much more susceptible of influence than the rustics.

Lady Byron continues in a further letter of 8th. December 1853

With this letter you will receive a Brighton Paper with an account of Mr. Tower's farewell to his parish and I wish that paragraph to be read by the Elmesthorpe tenants and circulated amongst the Shilton people that they may know how much beloved Mr. Tower was after nearly ten years ministering in a parish of the same extent, as to the population, as Earl Shilton.

Lady Byron had now to deal with the vacancy at Kirkby Mallory, and it must be mentioned here that if she had simply wanted to give Tower a 'comfortable' job then she would have presented him to the living at Kirkby. By taking on the new parish of Earl Shilton, Tower was taking on a tough challenge. However, in September 1853 Tower was out of a job. Lady Byron did appoint him Rector of Kirkby Mallory but he only occupied this office until the legal formalities of setting up the new parish had been completed in April 1854, although it is almost certain he never went to Kirkby in an official capacity during these few months particularly as Longhurst was still living at the rectory. Indeed Tower does not appear in the list of rectors of Kirkby which hangs in the church and it is quite likely that no one locally, apart from Charles Noel, was aware of the appointment which as we have seen lasted only for about six months.

Because of this, certain documents show the Rev. Thomas Noel as Rector until 1854 and give this year as the date of his death when as previously stated he died on 22nd. August 1853. Longhurst finally left the parish on 19th. April 1854. In addition to Kirkby and Earl Shilton, Lady Byron had another appointment to make following the death of the Rev. Thomas Noel. It is recorded that in early 1854 the Rev. Thomas Badcock was instituted to the vicarage of Fleckney by the Lord Bishop of Peterborough on the presentation of the Rt. Hon Baroness Noel Byron.

A letter from Lady Byron to Charles Noel dated 29th. September 1853 indicates that Longhurst had asked about the Fleckney vacancy but her advice to Charles was as follows:-

I think you must conclude on reflection that to keep any connection with the Longhurst family would only entail further trouble. Besides I hope to place a superior man at Fleckney. You had better let Longhurst know that the matter is otherwise determined, and not keep him in suspense.

Tower then became the first Vicar of Earl Shilton and Rector of Elmesthorpe. He was a single man and he immediately became involved in every aspect of village life. Money for the creation of the new parish came from various sources; among them was a gift by deed under trustees from Lady Byron of £500 which provided for the interest to be given to the minister of the parish. The Incorporated Society for the Promoting, Enlargement, Building and Repairing of Churches and Chapels voted a grant for rebuilding the church in July 1854. An amount of £600 was subscribed by the inhabitants of the Parish which Tower records with pride. Lady Byron contributed a further £200 saying to Charles Noel,

> *Pray ask Mr. Tower where he wishes my £200 subscription towards Earl Shilton Church to be paid-I will place the money in the bank for you to pay. The repairs of Earl Shilton Church will require a large sum and I must I believe head the subscriptions. Who are the landowners from whom contributions towards that project should be looked for?*

It was on the 18th. March 1854 that Tower first arrived officially in Earl Shilton. He recalled that when he first set foot in the old church the first person he saw there was a drunken man. In less than eighteen months the foundation stone of the rebuilt Church had been laid, on the 16th. August 1855. Fortunately reporters were present and the press report of the ceremony was as follows:

> *Laying of the Foundation Stone of the New Church at Earl's Shilton - The first stone of the church to be erected for the new parish of Earl's Shilton was laid yesterday by the Right Honourable the Earl Howe.*
> *The former church consisted of a chancel, with a chantry on the north side opening to the chancel with two arches, a nave with north aisle connected by an arcade of three arches, and a western tower and spire. To meet the requirements of an increasing population, it became necessary to enlarge the church, and to do so most effectually, the chancel and chantry, nave and aisle, which were found in a dangerous state, have been pulled down, and in their place a more extensive building is to be raised. The work pulled down was chiefly of the early part of the thirteenth century. The tower, with its stone crocketted spire, is of the fifteenth century, and of good proportions. The new building will consist of a chancel with north and south chantries, nave with north and south aisles and porches. The design is by the late Mr. R.C.Carpenter, of London, and under the superintendence of Mr. W.Slater, and is in the style of architecture which prevailed in the reign of Edward I - that is, about A.D. 1300, the best period of English architecture. As far as circumstances would permit, the idea of the ancient structure has been preserved. The chantry on the north side, with its two arches opening to the chancel, is reproduced and repeated on the south side. The nave is extended to five arches in length, and the width is such as to*

require a covering of three gabled roofs. The chancel is divided from the nave by a proper chancel arch, and extends about fifteen feet eastward of the chantries. The east window is filled with rich tracery, and is of five lights; the side windows are of two lights, with several varieties of tracery, which have been adopted from another church in the same parish, now in ruins. The roofs are of open timber work, covered with tiles. The walls are constructed of stone obtained in the parish, and a pleasing variety is derived from using the different coloured stones, which are procured in ornamental patterns. The windows are of Ancaster stone, and the arcades of Hollington stone. The work is proceeding under the direction of Mr. W.Slater (the late Mr. Carpenter's pupil and successor), architect, of 4, Carlton Chambers, Regent Street, London. The contractor is Mr. Rushin, of Leicester. The church will accommodate 800 persons, and the expense incurred will be about £3,000.

Every preparation was made in the village to celebrate the occasion in a fitting manner. Great numbers of persons from the neighbouring villages were present, as well as many from a distance. Besides the Earl and Countess Howe, there were present the Revs. T.Jones (of Leicester), E.T.Vaughan, G.E.Gillett, W.W.Greenway, H.K.Richardson, H.Homer, J.H.Scott, J.P.Newby, F.Merewether, and numerous other clergymen, whose names we did not ascertain.

The services of the day commenced with the administration of Holy Communion at an early hour, to which succeeded a short service at half-past eleven o'clock, when the Rev. R.T.Vaughan, assisted by the Rev. E. Tower, the incumbent, read prayers. and the Rev. G.E.Gillett preached, with his usual ability, from Isaiah, 1ii, 10- " The Lord hath made bare His holy arm in the eyes of the nations, and all the ends of the earth shall see the salvation of our God."

At the conclusion of this service, performed in the building used as a temporary church, a procession was formed, which moved forward, chanting appropriate psalms, to the site of the new building. On reaching the ground, on which spacious galleries were erected for the accommodation of spectators, and crowded by hundreds of persons, the Rev. G.E.Bruxner read Ephesians ii. 19 to the end, after which the Rev. E.Tower recited a prayer for the occasion.

The Nicene Creed was then recited, and Earl Howe having received from the architect the implements of the work, proceeded to lay the stone with the usual formalities, with the words:-

In the faith of our only Lord and Saviour Jesus Christ, we fix this stone on this foundation, in the name of the Father and of the Son and of the Holy Ghost;

that within these walls thereon to be raised bearing the name of Saint Simon and Saint Jude, and the pure Word of God may be preached and the Sacraments rightly and duly administered; and that this House of God may for ever be devoted to faithful prayer and holy praise, and to the edification and perfecting of disciples to the honour and praise of our Lord Jesus Christ, who with the Father and the Holy Ghost liveth and reigneth ever one God, world without end. Amen.

Underneath the stone was placed a copy of the Book of Common Prayer, a florin, and a slab bearing the following inscription :-

This Church,
Dedicated to the honour of S.S.Simon and Jude
Was rebuilt in the year of our Lord God 1855
The foundation stone was laid by
The Right Hon. Earl Howe, Aug. 16th. of the same year, in the reign of Queen Victoria.
George Davys, D.D.Bishop of the Diocese of Peterborough;
Ferdinand Ernest Tower, Perpetual Curate of the Parish;
Thomas Spencer and John Homer,Churchwardens;
R.C.Carpenter, and William Slater, his successor, Architects;
William Rushin, Builder.
Joseph Yates, Master Mason.
William Tookey, Clerk of the Works.

The stone having been lowered into its place, the Te Deum was sung and several collects recited, including a prayer for the workmen employed in the building, that they might be preserved from danger during the progress of the work. The service concluded by singing the Old Hundredth Psalm.

The Company present then adjourned to a commodious booth erected by Mr. Rushin, in a field adjoining the Bowling Green Inn, and superbly decorated with flowers and evergreens to partake of luncheon.

A number of toasts were given after luncheon, but as the reporters were not allowed to occupy seats within hearing of the speakers, although they had previously engaged them, we are sorry to be under the necessity of passing over this part of the proceedings in silence.

The church at Elmesthorpe, which it is proposed to restore, was visited in the afternoon, and Divine service was held again in the evening, when a sermon was preached by the Rev. H.K.Richardson, of Leire.

What a shame that the reporters could not hear all of the proceedings as stated in the penultimate paragraph; we shall now never know what tribute was paid to Lady Byron or if the party toasted her health. This report appeared in an old Parish magazine which the writer has in his possession.

Things were now moving quickly and in less than a year the new church was ready and a day of special services was held to celebrate the event on Friday 4th. July 1856.

At the morning service the sermon was preached by Doctor Hook of Leeds from John VI verse 10 and the choir under the direction of Mr. Reynolds, the village schoolmaster, performed the musical part of the service with much credit. The congregation for this service numbered about 200.

The preacher for the afternoon service was the Ven. Archdeacon Bickersteth on Matthew VI verse 9 and this was followed by another service at 5p.m. which was attended by over 600 persons 'mainly the poor and school children.'

The evening service attracted a large congregation and prayers were read by the Rev. G.E.Bruxner, Rector and Patron of the living at Thurlaston, who as mentioned previously was the principal person in touch with Lady Byron concerning the parish of Earl Shilton. Tower himself preached the sermon on 1st. Book of the Chronicles chapter 29 verse 2. The choir of St. Martin's Church, Leicester (now Leicester Cathedral) attended this service and 'gave great satisfaction to those present', as the report in the *Leicestershire Mercury* commented.

Many visitors from neighbouring villages attended these services including Mr. Thomas Cope, the high sheriff, and Mr. Christopher Tower, father of the Rev. Tower, and members of his family. Collections for the day totalled £137-3-9d.

It must have been a wonderful spectacle with dozens of carriages arriving in the village all day bringing the guests dressed in all their finery. The contrast with those poor people arriving for the 5p.m. service would be very apparent, but such differences were generally accepted. Tower would have been very pleased with the large attendance, and like Robertson, he would pursue the process of bringing the different sections of society together. It would appear from the numbers quoted that something approaching half the population of the village were present at the services on this day.

The next projects were to be the new church schools and a new vicarage. Lady Byron was kept informed by Tower of the progress. Writing to Charles Noel she says-

> *I will give up my school there as he will establish schools on a larger scale and more Church than I could enter into- so by leaving the field clear to him I shall avoid all collision. I will support other schools by the means withdrawn. I think that schools sanctioned by a Clergyman of known authority will prosper more than mine.*

In another letter to Charles Noel she emphasises this point-

> *I must as I told you keep clear of all concerns in the Parish of Earl Shilton, and I desire to leave Mr. Tower the entire management of the schools-so take care not to agree on my part to any arrangement either affirmative or negative about them- but leave him to his own plans. I have promised to assist in obtaining land for his school because that involves no question.*

The new school would, of course, be 'Church of England'. Such schools were being introduced at this time throughout the country. Having provided the means for this to happen, Lady Byron's participation was at an end.

A large piece of ground was purchased on the opposite side of the Hall Field from the Church. By the end of 1858 the new schools had been erected and by 1859 the vicarage was ready for the new Vicar, the cost of the former is stated at £1050 and the latter £1000, although another report says £1400. Some of the finance for these projects came from 'Queen Anne's Bounty' and there are a number of letters on this subject in the *Lovelace Byron Papers* between Lady Byron and Tower.

As well as dealing with bricks and mortar, Tower was attending to the welfare of the parish. Mr. George Foster, the Earl Shilton historian, who in his youth knew many people who remembered the period well, tells that soup kitchens were opened up at the vicarage and other meals were provided free or at moderate charge.

There are many letters in the *Lovelace Byron Papers* from Tower to Lady Byron on how he was tackling the subject of poverty in the village. In one interesting letter he tells Lady Byron that the poor people of the village are asked to pay two shillings and twopence for one stone of barleymeal at Earl Shilton but how each week they walk to the next village of Thurlaston where it can be bought for one shilling and eightpence. Tower obtained prices for other goods, particularly foodstuffs from other areas, bought them in bulk, and distributed them to the poor from the vicarage. All this detailed information was supplied by Tower to Lady Byron which shows the personal interest which she took in the projects to improve the welfare of the poor of the village.

Tower was shocked to find many couples living together unmarried and he promptly married them. He took it upon himself to intervene in trade disputes of which there were many, particularly a very bitter one in 1859 involving the Earl Shilton manufacturers Homer and Everard over pricing and frame rents. Taking an even-handed approach on the surface, Tower had the interests of the workers at heart and his remark on disputes is well worth repeating: 'Excess of obedience and forbearance is not to be expected from hungry men.'

No doubt though that Tower remembered the accusations levelled at Robertson back in Brighton of being a 'Socialist' and he would not have wanted to become embroiled in such controversy which might have brought out his former association and the Vicar of Brighton's veto. It has to be remembered that for several years after his death, Robertson was periodically being attacked by certain newspapers for his outspoken views and Robertson's father was called upon to defend his son's reputation. One letter from Tower to Lady Byron informs her that he was about to pay a visit to Robertson's family and possibly this subject was on the agenda.

It would have been very pleasing to be able to discover some connection between Tower and sport in Earl Shilton but nothing has come to hand. We know that he was a personal friend of Canon A.O.James who during his long life was a curate at nearby Stoney Stanton, Narborough with Huncote and Hinckley, before becoming a Canon of St. Martins, Leicester. Canon James played cricket for Sparkenhoe Rovers and was regarded as an excellent all-rounder, playing against Earl Shilton on a number of occasions. The only sporting connection that is known is that Tower gained a rowing blue at Cambridge University in 1842 which according to reports was the last time that the crew rowed in top hats! As an afterthought perhaps his energy was fully used on parish duties.

Lady Byron's daughter. Ada, Countess of Lovelace

CHAPTER SEVEN

Lady Byron - The Last Decade

As we have seen, the decade 1850-60 saw Earl Shilton move from the ancient into the modern. For Lady Byron also it was to be her final decade. She died on the 16th. May 1860 one day before her 68th. birthday.

In June 1851, over the Whitsuntide festival, Lady Byron visited Leicestershire and the following is a report from the *Leicester Journal* of the visit witnessed by their correspondent. Headed 'Kindness of Lady Byron'.

To the Editor - Sir
We sometimes have it sounded in our ears that 'Man's inhumanity to man makes countless thousands mourn,' and we are too often impressed with the truth of this poetic infusion by what we feel and see passing around us; but I am happy in having the pleasure of informing your readers that the inhabitants of this populous village have had another opportunity of enjoying the munificence of that highly honoured and much respected lady, whose name is always associated with deeds of benevolence, and of whom it may truly be said that she 'goes about doing good.' During the last fortnight nearly 200 hands have been employed on the estate of Lady Noel Byron, at Kirkby and Elmesthorpe, at digging the fallows, stocking up on roots etc. On Saturday her ladyship took occasion to address about 30 of the men thus employed, when they went to receive their wages, on frugality, economy, the advantages of knowledge, and the powerful influences of human kindness. On the latter her ladyship expatiated much; she spoke very feelingly, and followed up her advice by subsequent acts of practical kindness. On Monday there was a tea drinking at the Moats, and although the weather rendered it unfavourable for distant visitors, there were several hundreds assembled from the villages for miles around, who all partook of tea, coffee, or some kind of refreshment, provided at

Lady Byron's expense. Her ladyship passed through Shilton this morning, and I should think the oldest man living in the village had never witnessed such manifestations of respect and gratitude as was shown to that kind hearted lady on that occasion. Wreaths of flowers were strung together, extending from one side of the street to the other; garlands and bowers were made; and every expression of respect which could be given was cheerfully bestowed upon her. Many sums of money have been distributed among the large families this morning, from the same bountiful source. One proposition which her ladyship made to the working men of Shilton must not be forgotten as it is perhaps one of the most important ever submitted to them. It is to give them a bonus of 10 per cent on all monies which they will place in her hands during the next twelve months. If working men will but avail themselves of this noble offer, it will be greatly to their interest. The working classes have yet to learn the lessons of self-reliance. There is a power within themselves which, when fully appreciated and properly wrought out, will secure to them a place in society, not of the meanest kind. I am sir your obliged servant A CORRESPONDENT, Earl Shilton, June 16th, 1851.

The *Leicestershire Mercury* carried a similar description of events. A further report in this newspaper at this time was as follows.

Anniversary- The members of a Friendly Society meeting at the Plough Inn, held their anniversary on Whit Tuesday, when an excellent substantial dinner was provided by the host and hostess. Both at and after dinner Mr.Fulshaw (surgeon to the society) was in the chair, and one of the chief sentiments of the evening was the health of Lady Byron, with thanks to her for the interest she evinces in the depressed condition of the framework knitters of Earl Shilton, and accompanied by the remark that, this is not the first occasion on which her ladyship has taken similar steps to relieve the working classes of Earl Shilton. A vote of thanks was also coupled with the health of Mr.Noel, for so warmly carrying out the benevolent views of Lady Byron; and a hearty wish was added that others similarly favoured by Providence would follow these noble and excellent examples. The afternoon and evening were spent in a most agreeable manner, several spirited songs and glees being contributed by the Chairman, and Messrs. Ball, Whitmore, Forster etc. One of the first songs, but this was before Lady Byron's health was drunk, was 'Women shall never wear the breeches' being selected, we imagine to show that women can rule her so-called lords better by the exercise of her kind and loving qualities than by competing with him for supremacy in the political arena.

Lady Byron's signature
Deed of the Manor of Earl Shilton to Lady Byron as a lessee of the Queen, 1849

Sampler worked at Lady Byron's School, Earl Shilton by Evelena Rowley Foster

What would Lady Byron's reaction have been to this report, I wonder?

During Lady Byron's visit to Earl Shilton she visited her school and reviewed the work of the pupils. She was so impressed by the sampler worked by Evelena Rowley Foster, mentioned earlier, that she presented her with ten shillings as a reward for her good work.

Following the death of her only daughter Augusta Ada, Countess of Lovelace, in 1852, Lady Byron had erected a monument on the border of Kirkby Mallory churchyard not actually on consecrated ground. Ada, at her own request, had been buried in the Byron vault at Hucknall parish church in Nottinghamshire, but appears to have requested that a monument be placed at Kirkby.

After her visit in 1851, I have not been able to trace any record of Lady Byron coming to Leicestershire again. She may then have never seen or read the wording on the monument although she certainly chose the text, because it clearly states Ada's birth date as being 10th. December 1816 when in actual fact it should have read 1815. It is quite likely that this error occurred because of the entry in the baptismal register at Kirkby on 2nd. November 1816 nearly one year after her first baptism in London in December 1815.

It also shows the name as Ada Augusta and not Augusta Ada as she was christened. Whether this was to Lady Byron's instructions or simply the architect or engraver recording her as she was known I do not know.

An account advising on this monument from James M.Lockyer of 19 Southampton Street, Fitzroy Square, London for £30-19-0 is filed in the *Lovelace Byron Papers*. The error in Ada's birth date while not of great importance in itself, is unfortunate as it tends to be taken as fact by writers on this subject.

To mark Ada's burial next to her father in the Byron vault, the following interesting poem was written and published by Joseph J.Hadley in the *Leicester Journal*

The Grave of Byron by Joseph J.Hadley

Here, then, he rests! and broken is the lyre,
Whose swelling numbers rolled in ceaseless song,
And o'er his grave the voices of the quire,
When Sabbath brings again the wonted throng
Of village worshippers, flout solemnly and slow,
Unheard by him who in deep silence sleeps below.

And there he sleeps! unconscious that the brave
And fair, and good, and wise, in turn appear
Within these walls, and ponder o'er his grave,
And to his memory shed the votive tear.
The heart cynic's sneer, the love-lorn maiden's sigh
Alike unheard by him, both pass unheeded by,

And not the rustic villagers alone,
When the full anthem swells through arch and aisle,
Assemble here, but men from every zone,
Are often seen within the ancient pile,
From each far distant land the toil - worn pilgrims come
Their homage pure to pay at hapless Harold's tomb.

And there he lies among his kindred dust,
His earthly essence fleeting fast away
His once bright coronet obscured by rust
His body to ignoble worms a prey,
Through the corrupting mass his noble name we trace
Yet feel that Time's stern hand this record will efface.

But lo ! the greedy tomb its jaws extends,
The deep-toned bell booms loudly on the air
With sable pomp a long procession wends
Its mournful course into the house of prayer:
In the wide yawning gulf with heartfelt tears they place
The lovliest and last of that deed enobled race.

And now, behold! reposing by his side
His well - loved daughter! Ada his sole child.
May fitly by her father's bones abide;
Upon the old ancestral coffins piled,
Byron with Lovelace tranquil sleeps: the child and sire
"Ashes to Ashes" joined, a closer bond acquire.

The obsequies are over, and the throng
In silence enter the abode of death,
And not a few are fain to linger long;

With awe and sorrow, and with baited breath,
I peer into the gloomy sepulchre and turn
My mournful gaze on those the frowning walls intern.

Do my eyes wrong me? have we pilferers here?
Is sacrilege no crime - is virtue fled?
Dispoilers of the tomb ! have ye no fear
That some avenging bolt may strike ye dead?
That form, though senseless now, again with life shall beat,
And charge ye with the crime before the judgment seat.

Close, close the tomb ! once more shut out the day
From the dank vault, let no one enter there,
Let not presumptuous men remove away
Those sacred relics which old Time may spare.
Let Harold rest in peace ! warm tears from gentle eyes
Shall ever mark the spot where our great poet lies.

I have not been able to discover any information on Mr. Hadley, but the poem was printed in the *Leicester Journal*, a weekly poem being a feature of this newspaper.

It is most interesting to recall that Ada died aged 36 – Byron and his father both died at this age.

Lady Byron was concerned that the reduction in the value of the benefice of Kirkby Mallory because of the division of the parishes would affect her plans. In a letter to Charles Noel dated 6th September she stated that she wanted someone with at least ten years experience, plain overt preachings, and active personal interest in the parishioners without strong party views of any kind, and that she had some idea of who she wanted but was not sure as she had never heard him preach. Presumably it was Samuel Gamlen because letters are very quickly exchanged on the subject.

Lady Byron wrote to Charles Noel about her own school in Earl Shilton:

I wish to know what is the expense per head in round numbers of my Shilton School which I wish to have turned into a nice garden when the large schools are established by Mr Tower.

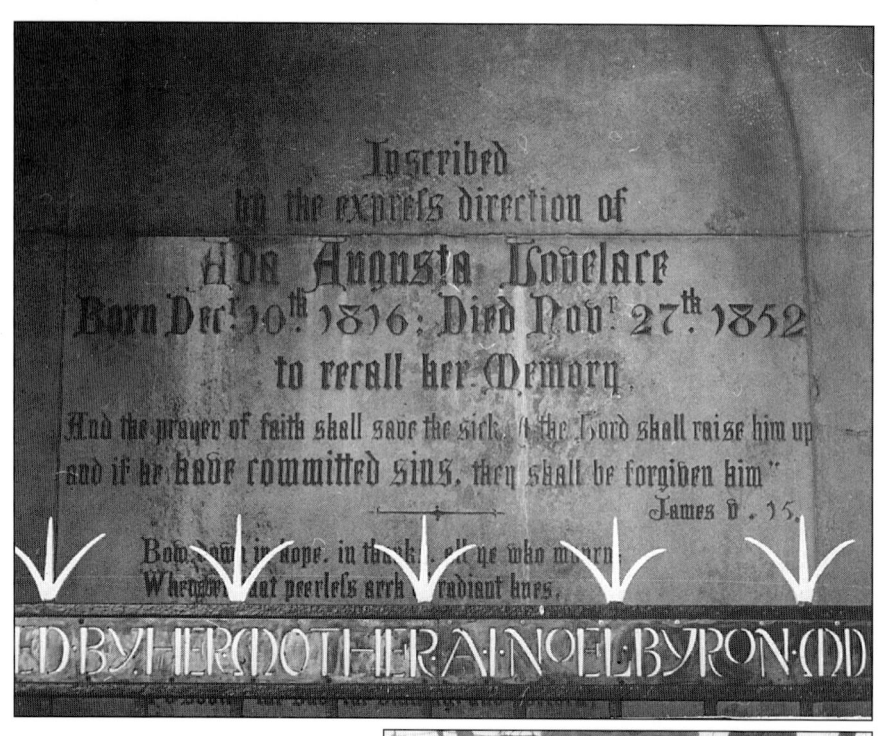

> Inscribed
> by the express direction of
> Ada Augusta Lovelace
> Born Dec.r 10th 1816; Died Nov.r 27th 1852
> to recall her Memory.
>
> "And the prayer of faith shall save the sick, & the Lord shall raise him up
> and if he have committed sins, they shall be forgiven him"
> James v. 15.
>
> Bow down in hope, in thanks, all ye who mourn;
> Where'er that peerless arch of radiant hues...
>
> ED BY HER MOTHER A. NOEL BYRON. MD

Section of the monument to Ada at the edge of Kirkby churchyard showing incorrect year of birth. It should have read 1815 not 1816

Right: full monument

Later in 1854 she writes:

> As I contribute otherwise to Mr Tower's Schools, I do not mean to leave the wooden and iron rooms at Earl Shilton - but it requires some consideration where they could best be placed. My first object would be to have the children within the Parish of Kirkby on account of Mr Gamlen's influence - I would certainly not have any kind of school in Mr Cooper's Parish (Peckleton) - therefore consider what spot would be likely to unite the Peckleton and Kirkby children. I forget whether the parishes are divided by the stream at the entrance to Peckleton or nearer Kirkby. It is also a question whether the two rooms would not be more useful together... You might send me a sketch of any situation that appeals suitable to you and Mr Gamlen.

I cannot say for certain just where these wooden and iron buildings were situated in Earl Shilton, but there is a strong possibility that they were just inside West Street, near to what is now the Working Mens Club. This open area of land has been used by pupils at the Church of England schools for gardening for as long as anyone living can remember. This would have fulfilled Lady Byron's wish that the land should be used as a garden.

It is very rewarding to read these many letters to Tower and Charles Noel which illustrate the great personal interest Lady Byron took in these projects. Besides her enormous financial contributions, she displays a warmth and understanding when dealing with the problems and her caring and attentive attitude is clearly evident.

Sometime during the 1850's Charles Noel appears to have vacated Peckleton House and removed to Hinckley spending some time at Leamington Spa. In 1856 the Leicestershire Juvenile Reformatory was founded on land around this site with Earl Howe as its president. Lady Byron who owned Peckleton House gave full support to this project as contained in the following report:

> The farm has undergone no change since the last report. You were informed that 18 acres had been rented in addition to the 12 acres of grass land which together with Peckleton House Lady Noel Byron so generously placed for a term of years at the disposal of the Institution

Charles Noel and his wife Mary had done much to help the poor and needy but in 1857 both he and his wife met a tragic death from smallpox. Once again

Lady Byron had lost a friend and above all someone she could trust. Lady Byron wrote to her tenants to inform them of the sad loss and a memorial service was held at the Hinckley Great Meeting Unitarian Chapel and a tablet to commemorate their work was placed on the wall of the Church. The Rev Hugh Hutton travelled from London specially to conduct this memorial service. Charles had originally joined the navy for a short time and then considered taking up holy orders but finally he chose to become Lady Byron's land agent for which he appeared eminently suited. It is sad to relate that when his father the Rev Thomas Noel died in 1853 it was discovered that Charles had been excluded from his will presumably because of his lifelong association with Lady Byron, but to the great credit of his brothers and sisters they agreed amongst themselves that Charles would get his share.

After the brief appointment of Tower as Rector of Kirkby Mallory, Lady Byron appointed the Rev. Samuel Gamlen as Rector in 1854 followed by the Rev John Young in the following year 1855.

Changes taking place in the industry can be illustrated in the 1850's through a look at the life of Mr. Job Toon. In 1850 he was a grocer and licensed victualler at Earl Shilton. He was a deeply religious Methodist and was therefore urged to give up the sale of alcoholic beverages which he did although continuing for several years as a grocer. He then invested in the purchase of a stocking frame which was worked from his home by his family. His business knowledge led him to buying further frames which he rented out and then marketed the products to traders and merchants in Leicester. This would be done by carrier's cart making the ten mile journey, but the 1860's were to see the full opening of the Leicester, Nuneaton and Birmingham railway line. In 1864 there was a convenient station at Elmesthorpe some one and a half miles from Earl Shilton which enabled rapid transport to the rest of the country and indeed to many countries overseas. The business continued to prosper. Gradually the knitters ceased to work in their own homes and the factory system took over. At first the factory used steam power but soon after switched to gas. The Earl Shilton Gas Light and Coke Company built its gas works in 1866 on a site off what is now Station Road, the opening ceremony being performed by the Rev. Tower. Gradually Toon and later his children and grandchildren were able to expand the business which was to become one of the largest employers in the area. (Known as the 'Premier' Works). Sadly soon after celebrating its centenary in 1950, J. Toon and Sons Ltd. ceased to trade and the large factory in Wood Street, after passing through a number of different owners was demolished in the 1980's.

With the coming of the factory system many of the old evils were eradicated such as child labour and unsuitable working conditions and general exploitation, but first the previously mentioned Cotton Famine was to hit the area with great severity. The American Civil War resulted in a blockade of the ports belonging to the Southern States which in turn prevented raw materials reaching this country. A large percentage of the village had no work. Many families had no alternative but to take refuge in the Hinckley Workhouse, commonly referred to as 'The Bastille'.

Once again a huge relief operation took place and Tower immediately took up the cause of his parishioners as the following article from the *Leicester Journal* illustrates.

While we are urging the claims of Lancashire upon the benevolent public, we are startled by the voice of distress, even at our own doors. The letter from our correspondent, the incumbent of Earl's Shilton (Tower always put apostrophes on the village name) shows that in the neighbourhood of Hinckley the distress caused by the cotton famine is probably as great as elsewhere; but for the fact that the poor framework knitters of that locality have never known the prosperity of Lancashire, the pinch they now have to endure is submitted to without a murmur although we believe the pressure to be as severe and equally deserving help. Whatever may be thought of the scheme proposed by our Rev. correspondent we think that our Relief Committee would do well to consider how far it is desirable to help their own neighbours. The fund is raised for the relief of the cotton districts and we see no reason why a portion of it should not be applied in mitigating the distress which exists among the framework knitters of Hinckley and its neighbourhood.

Leicester Journal November 28th. 1862

From a balance sheet published in 1864 the City of Leicester is shown as contributing £615-15s-7d out of a total of £6080-3s-10d raised locally and throughout the country. It is worth recording here that not all of the money raised was distributed and the balance was used to help finance the new Hinckley Public Library in 1871.

Lady Byron's charitable contributions following her death, we are informed by Tower, were taken up by her son-in-law the Earl of Lovelace and his daughter Lady Anne Isabella Noel. She was later to become Baroness Wentworth and was named, of course, after her grandmother Lady Byron.

J Toon & Sons Ltd. Earl Shilton factories – about 1880 (above) and 1950 (below)

The new railway station at Elmesthorpe although only one and a half miles away from Earl Shilton was not easily accessible. The only respectable road to Elmesthorpe from Earl Shilton was the present Elmesthorpe Lane, a continuation of the road from Barwell, which meant a lengthy detour from the village centre. The present day Station Road was then known as Breach Lane and then only extended along the line of the present Station Road to a sand and gravel pit near the parish boundary with Elmesthorpe. What is now known as Wilkinson's Lane, Elmesthorpe did not exist as a road or even, it seems, a footpath.

The land owned by Lady Byron until her death now belonged to Lord

Lovelace and he agreed to the new public road being built across his land. This road to Elmesthorpe is a continuing tribute to the hundreds of workpeople, destitute because of the cotton famine, who built the road. A small sum of money was paid to the workers plus provisions in the form of bread and meat. Much land in Elmesthorpe had already been drained on the instructions of Lady Byron to make it suitable for smallholdings and this process continued after her death.

It is interesting to record here the obituary for Lady Byron printed by the *Leicester Journal*. It confirms that estimation of her character which we have found so much in evidence.

> *We much regret to announce the decease of this distinguished Lady whose loss will be severely felt by a large circle of relatives and friends as well as by her tenantry and the poorer classes. Her Ladyship has long been known for her enlightened benevolence and her efforts to promote the education and moral improvement of her fellow creatures.*
>
> *There are few charities in this county to which she did not liberally subscribe and the conspicuous part which she took in the Reformatory Movement by gratuitously giving up a house and land at Peckleton to the cause entitle her to a place amongst the principal philanthropists of the age.*
>
> *The funeral of the late Lady Noel Byron took place at noon on Monday last at Kensall Green Cemetery and was attended by her two youngest grandchildren, Lady Anne and the Hon. Ralph King, Miss Montgomery, Lord and the Hon. F. Byron, The Rt. Hon Dr Lushington, The Rev Mr Burton, Mr Ford and Mr C. Smith.*
>
> *An entire absence of ostentation characteristic of the taste of the deceased prevailed throughout the funeral arrangements-neither coronet nor escutcheons were to be seen and simply her name was inscribed on the plain oaken coffin. Since our recent notice of her Ladyship's death further losses in the cause of charity have become known to us. Other schools and institutions than those at Kirkby were solely maintained by her, and a reformatory for females at Bristol was erected and supported by her own charge.*

Another report is headed 'Lady Byron and the Garibaldi Fund' and the following letter from the committee of that fund was published:

> *Sir, We owe a debt of gratitude to the memory of Lady Noel Byron which we hope you will allow us to discharge by means of your valuable paper. A few days*

before her death Lady Byron turning a sympathising thought to Italy sent £40 as a subscription to the Garibaldi Fund, accompanying the gift with heartfelt wishes for the cause of the country. We consider this act from such a person on the eve of her departure from the struggles of this world a favourable omen to the Italian hopes, a blessing to the heroes who are now fighting not for any selfish aim or reward but to open the way to a generous race shamefully downtrodden by a godless tyranny to assert its noblest privileges among the nations. Lady Byron appears to have thought in her dying hour that the name she bore was a symbol of deathless harmony between the English and Italian mind and the spirit of the great bard of 'Childe Harold' seems to have been with her etc...

Let those who criticise her for being self-centred, unforgiving, intransigent etc. be aware of the facts set out here, and perhaps give credit where it is due. It is true that she was a rich woman and the money she donated to dozens of causes, not forgetting the Leicester Royal Infirmary, would not have been a particular burden to her. The important thing is that she did give generously and she did have compassion and she did care, and she did her best to improve the lot of her fellow human beings.

One last point which readers should appreciate is that Lady Byron did not attend the funeral of her husband in 1824 or the funeral of her daughter Ada in 1852. She did not attend the laying of the foundation stone of the new church at Earl Shilton in 1855 or the service a year later to commemorate the opening. It was not unusual for this to happen in Victorian England and ladies were not expected to take part in such ceremonies. Lady Byron adhered willingly to this protocol.

Enough then has now been said to show something of Lady Byron's character. 'My days are numbered and my deeds recorded' wrote Byron in his great poem 'Manfred' - and may this apply also to Lady Byron!

CHAPTER EIGHT
The 'New' Earl Shilton

The new schools having been built by 1860 Tower was responsible for staff appointments in them. The Headmaster in 1859 was Mr. Samuel Reynolds who held this office until 1900. He was born in 1831 in Somerset and served even longer as Superintendent of the Church Sunday Schools, over 47 years. The next appointment was Miss Bucktin who commenced her duties here on 6th. January 1862 coming direct from Whitelands College in London. Miss Bucktin recalls her arrival in the parish- 'At that time the cotton famine greatly affected the parish as the staple employment then was framework knitting. The cotton famine was followed by one of the worst epidemics of fever that Shilton has experienced, scarcely a household escaping.'

Miss Bucktin spent much of her spare time visiting the fever cases in the parish. She later married Captain Speedy of the Mercantile Service and for a time they resided in Earl Shilton, the family being good friends with the Reynolds family. In 1923 in her eighties she paid a brief visit to Earl Shilton to meet old friends. Reynolds had a large family and lived in a house adjacent to the High Street Schools near where the present day Church Hall is built, next to the pathway leading to the church. This is always to this day known as 'Gaffers Alley' after him. Reynolds' daughter Amy married a Mr. H.R.Steer a well-known artist.

Changes were also taking place at Kirkby Mallory following Lady Byron's death. The poet Byron's cousin George Anson Byron had supported Lady Byron over the separation and had been friendly with her ever since. On the Poet's death he became the 7th. Lord Byron but no wealth came to him and Lady Byron herself was able to give him a helping hand. He was a Captain in the Navy. One of his many assignments was to command the ship 'Blonde' in

The Hon. and Rev. Augustus Byron

1824 for a special mission to the Sandwich Islands. The King and Queen of these Islands had been on a state visit to London where they fell ill with measles and died and it was his mission to return their bodies to their homeland for burial.

Our interest however is in his third son the Hon. and Rev. Augustus Byron who became Rector of Kirkby Mallory soon after Lady Byron's death, and was to hold that office from 1861 until his death on 17th. July 1907. With Tower at Earl Shilton and Byron at Kirkby Mallory for the two decades of the 1860's and 1870's they brought a great deal of stability to the parishes and seemed to have been good friends. I was fortunate some years ago to be able to meet Augustus Byron's grandson, Mr. Aubrey Moore, who was then in his nineties and had seen his grandfather as a boy. I learned how the Rev. Byron appeared to act not only as Minister, but as lawyer, doctor, teacher and advisor to anyone who sought his help on any topic. Mr. Moore had a striking photograph of his grandfather headed 'Christs Faithful Soldier and Servant, Unto His Life's End' followed by an interesting poetic tribute:

A missed man in the country-side,
Where every labourer knew
His cheery call, as he passed them by
With the happy light in his clear grey eye:
And the greeting given to each and all
From cot or farmstead, or lordly hall
Alike frank, kind and true.

A missed man by the dying bed
Where he held the stiffening hand;
Patient watched through the fevered hour
Soothed and guided with words or power
Friend, physician and priest in one,
Help to the mourner when all was done
With the heart that could 'understand'.

A missed man in the grey old church
Where his majestic voice
To every litany, collect and prayer
Gave the soul their framer's had planted there
While he taught in language simple and clear
Our hope in heaven, our duty here
Bade man in God rejoice.

Missed in all social gatherings
Bright host and welcomed friend;
Missed by young and old and grave and gay,
Missed in his life-paths day by day;
Missed as men miss their truest and best
Loved and honoured, and mourned, and blest,
A missed man till the end.

The 7th. Lord Byron died in 1868 and is buried next to the monument to Ada in Kirkby Churchyard. His son the Rev. Augustus Byron is buried nearby as are several other members of the family.

The situation over the cotton famine was beginning to ease by 1864 and with the opening of the Leicester to Birmingham railway line that year trade was improving. Tower had now been in Earl Shilton for ten years. To celebrate this he wrote a paper on the history of the village which he presented to the Leicestershire Architectural and Archaeological Society on the 28th. March in that year. New machinery for the hosiery industry was being introduced as the factory system established itself, particularly that designed and built by William Cotton of Loughborough, and as stated previously the new gas works were officially opened by Tower in 1866. Tower was also involved in a body called 'The Twelve Parishes Labourers Friendly Society' which encouraged self reliance. A further indication of increasing prosperity within the village was the formation, in 1857, of the 'Earl Shilton Permanent Benefit Building and Land Society'. The *Leicester Journal* of 29th May 1857 said that this 'bids fair to benefit the labouring and industrious classes of the community' enabling them to purchase property being erected in the village. The first Chairman of the newly formed Society was Mr. John Homer, Churchwarden at that time. The first (part-time) Manager was the Reverend Michael Shore, Minister of the Baptist Church, and it is pleasing that the same 'Earl Shilton Building Society' still flourishes one hundred and forty years later, having played a large part in establishing home ownership within the village.

In 1861 Tower was living at the new vicarage employing a housekeeper, Maria Davies, to look after his domestic life. She was around 60 years old and was born at Ellesmere, Shropshire, but shortly afterwards he was to return to his former parish of Hurstpierpoint in Sussex to marry Miss Mary Georgina Campion of nearby Danny Park.

On his return to Earl Shilton, with his new wife, much work was still required to beautify the Church and Tower did much internal decoration himself, some of which can still be seen today and is being carefully restored. Mrs. Tower embroidered some of the altar cloths and frontals.

In 1864 the first of the Tower children was born and named Henry, followed by five brothers and two sisters. Henry was sent to Lancing College to be trained for the ministry under Canon Willard. He was there in November 1874 when his mother died at Earl Shilton. Apparently he was sent there earlier than was normal and suffered from bullying from the older boys. It was quite a harsh regime. Certainly he never forgot his experiences there, particularly the day he was called into the Head's study and informed of the death of his mother. No sympathy or comfort was offered to him and the memory of that dreadful moment remained with him for the rest of his life. After being ordained he took an appointment in Leicester for a short time before moving to Weedon in Northamptonshire as Rector in the 1890's. He then moved to Holy Trinity Church, Windsor in 1900 where he remained until after the Second World War dying in 1948.

Having achieved his first ambitions at Earl Shilton, Tower now turned his

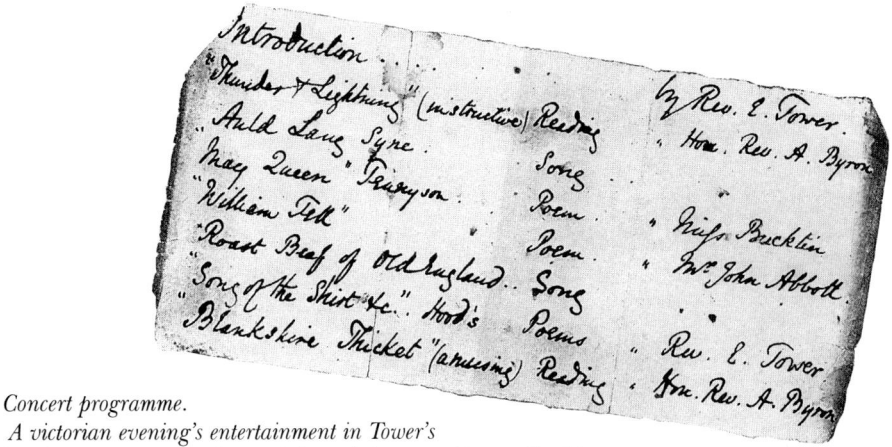

Concert programme.
A victorian evening's entertainment in Tower's handwriting. Tower, Miss Bucktin and Augustus Byron all taking part

attention to the small neighbouring parish of Elmesthorpe which was annexed to Earl Shilton.

The Church which had been a ruin for over a hundred years was re-opened for services on Tuesday 14th. July 1868. A report stated:

'The whole responsibility of the work undertaken has rested upon the Incumbent to whom we wish God's speed. The morning service began with the processional hymn- Christ is made the sure foundation - The prayers were intoned by the Hon. & Rev. A.Byron.'. The report goes on to say that Holy Communion was celebrated by the Rev. Tower, Rector, and that there were fifty communicants including the Clergy.

1868 saw the death not only of the 7th. Lord Byron but also that of William Swinney the old parish clerk who also ran the old ragged schools. At his funeral Tower was full of praise for his lifetime's work for the village and the Church and remarked that 'he had rather be a doorkeeper in the House of God than dwell in the tents of ungodliness'.

With W.E.Forster's Education Act of 1870 making education compulsory clearly more teachers were needed. This brought to Earl Shilton two ladies who were to have a great influence on the boys and girls of the village for the next forty years, in fact up until the end of the First World War.

Miss Elizabeth Jane Whitnell was appointed headmistress of the Infant school by Tower in 1875 immediately on leaving college. She remained in that office until her retirement in 1919. She died on 30th. July 1925 at the age of 71 at her sister's house in London and is buried in Wandsworth Cemetery.

Mrs Mary Georgina Tower

The Rev. Tower with children and domestic staff, Earl Shilton Vicarage 1874.

The Rev. Tower with his children at the grave of their mother, Earl Shilton Churchyard 1874

Miss Sarah Emma Walton was appointed a teacher at about the same time as Miss Whitnell. She was to remain a teacher here for the next 42 years before her death on 13th. October 1919 at the age of 64. Miss Walton is buried in Earl Shilton Churchyard and on her gravestone is inscribed a short memorial to Miss Whitnell. According to old residents they were very close friends during their life and the village wished them to be remembered together in death.

Being a Church of England school, when a teacher was appointed he or she was duty bound to play a full part in Church affairs. Both Miss Walton and Miss Whitnell were active in the Sunday Schools and other activities such as the Girls' Friendly Society. In addition, the Schools were always in need of money for their upkeep and expansion and many events took place to raise money for this purpose. The teachers would of course be required to assist in this process. On Friday 4th. July 1899 Miss Walton was presented with an Illuminated Address and Tea Service (from the well-known firm of Mappin & Webb) for having been Superintendent of the Girls Sunday School for fourteen years. Miss Walton was also teacher of a Bible class.

One other project was to be assigned to Tower during his time at Earl Shilton, in fact at the height of the cotton famine in 1862. He received a letter from the Rev. Stopford Brooke who was about to publish a biography of Robertson requesting his assessment of his friend's life for inclusion in this book. This was not an easy task for Tower to undertake because he must have been concerned that such a biography would raise again the humiliation he had been subjected to at Brighton. As far as can be ascertained no-one at Earl Shilton was aware of those events and he would not have wanted his achievements to have been undermined by such revelations.

In his reply to Brooke, Tower writes a wonderful tribute to his former colleague, but does not touch on the dispute with the Vicar of Brighton. This was fully in accordance with what he knew to be the wish of the departed Robertson. It was now a closed book.

Come the new decade of the 1880's Tower now a widower, must have felt that he had faithfully served the community for over twenty - five years. His wife, as mentioned previously had died in 1874, and was buried in Earl Shilton churchyard, where her grave can still be seen. Whether or not he had ever read Lady Byron's letter to Longhurst dated 7th. September 1853 quoted earlier we do not know but he had certainly justified her faith in him. To repeat the sentence from her letter with which the villagers past and present of Earl Shilton could identify fully endorses the action she took in that year.

'My sole consideration is the welfare of the Parish - and if I should not judge wisely with respect to the future Incumbent it will not be from the influence of private interest or feeling.'

Lady Byron did judge wisely and Tower will always be remembered with admiration and respect for his efforts to improve the lot of the villagers. It must be said that everyone connected with the village throughout the twentieth century has continued to enjoy the fruits of his labours and he certainly left the village in a much better state than he found it. He announced that he was leaving Earl Shilton to take up an appointment at Guildford and he invited his parishioners to meet him for a final time in the Church on Sunday 1st. January 1882. Tower chose for his final address to the large congregation the text that his friend Robertson had used on his final appearance in Trinity Chapel Brighton nearly thirty years earlier - 2nd. Book of Corinthians, Chapter Thirteen, Verse Eleven.

So ended the direct influence of Lady Byron and Ernest Tower on the affairs of Earl Shilton. Their input had created the climate for the village to achieve relative prosperity in the succeeding years. Unfortunately Tower was not to enjoy his new parish for very long as he died at St. Leonards-on-Sea on 20th. January 1885 of what we now know as leukaemia.

Tower's response to Brooke's request for his assessment and opinions of Robertson is now printed in full. This is followed by his final address to the people of Earl Shilton which was printed and distributed to the villagers at the time and was again reprinted by request in 1924 - this book would not be complete without it.

My Dear Sir - As I understand your letter, you ask me to add something to the materials now being collected for a 'Life of Robertson'. I wish I could send something worthy of such an object; but my incapability of writing all that I feel about him is my fair excuse for not giving more than what follows. It is right at the same time that I remind you that my friendship with him was, strictly speaking, a clerical friendship, and that he hardly ever spoke to me upon any other subject than that which directly or indirectly touched upon a clergyman's duties.

First of all, I will declare that, though he was not faultless any more than other human beings, he was without exception, the most faultless clergyman I have ever known. It is easy to trace how this comparative clerical faultlessness had its original spring - in (1) his strict obedience to his father's will that he should take Holy Orders and sacrifice the Army, in which his heart was; and (2) in his exceeding truthfulness of character. These two points ran through his life - Self - sacrifice and Truth. 'If I am to be a Clergyman', was the language of his thoughts, 'I will do my best to be a clergyman in reality, even though I have no preference for the profession.'

With this determination before him, he told me he prepared for ordination, and amongst other studies before he left college he literally learnt by heart the whole of the New Testament, not only in English but in Greek; and so completely did he devote himself to stiff theological study for the examination of the Bishop of Winchester, that he sought relaxation to his mind before the day of ordination by reading Wordsworth's 'Excursion' as his orisons. 'Some clergymen,' he said 'would think it strange to do this. It was my refreshment.'

His favourite private prayer book was Bishop Andrewes' 'Devotions,' which he used until he found his wants more perfectly expressed by the language of his own copiously flowing thoughts. His love for the Holy Bible was exceedingly remarkable, and especially for those parts which are (as he expressed it himself) full 'Christ' ; and it is worth recording that, upon one occasion, he remarked to me that the longer he lived the more fond he became of turning to the four Gospels by preference-a fact borne out by the list of his sermons.

But Robertson was pre-eminently the clergyman of thought. He would wring his very brain for the sake of those pure thoughts which abound throughout his writings. And yet it was not for the sake of exalting the intellect above religion that he did this, but in order to make the fullest use of the great faculties which God had blessed him withal. I was curate of Hurstpierpoint in 1851, and having at heart the opening of a parish reading-room, I applied to my friend to assist me with an address. His generosity encouraged the request, but it was with difficulty that I could prevail upon him to sacrifice any time from his congregation. 'My congregation must come first' he repeated: and then he rapidly sketched the amount of work which was demanded of him, in order that I might understand his sermons to be the chief object of his work- not his lectures, because intellect ought to bend to Christianity.

I am not fulsome in my language of him, when I say that the spirit of Christ saturated everything he said and did. For my own part, I have never learnt so much of the mind of Christ, and what is meant by following Christ, as from him. Like his Master (as he fearlessly loved to call the Saviour, in whatever company he was) he had two distinct sides to his character. Perfectly conscious of his great mental powers, and very modest about introducing them except where plain duty obliged him, he was ready to acknowledge excellence and rarity of endowments in everyone who possessed them, and to judge of others who had them not in a kindly spirit. There was a daring in him to speak what he was persuaded was the truth, which was quite unsubject to the good or bad opinions of the world. Yet this fearlessness was always governed by a most generous charity. If he mentioned the name of anyone whose life offended him, he was sure to make me see the good in the person as well as the vice. If he spoke of anyone who differed with him in religion, he was bent upon my seeing that he loved the individual while he hated his false faith. To the Church of England he was affectionately attached: he regarded it as the best form of Christianity in the world, but he would never refuse to recognise what was true and good in those outside it. I well remember the substance of his words in conversation with me on this point:- 'There is only one thing we have to wage a perpetual war with - sin and wrong, in whomsoever found- Churchman, Roman Catholic, or Protestant Dissenter. There is only one thing we should wish to see either in ourselves or in others - the love of Christ; and in whomsoever a spark merely of this love is found, whether in one whom we have regarded as awfully wicked, or in one whom we have looked on as not enjoying the same superior light with ourselves- one branded by the hard name of Papist, or a Greek, or a Dissenter, or an Arian; if in any of these the love of Christ is found, showing itself in the adoration and the worship of Him', - and then, I remember well, he added, with a tone which has fixed these words exactly upon my memory, 'oh, if I could adore Him and love Him and serve Him as some of these do, I should be a different person to what I am now ! Then, while we hold fast our own opinion and be ready to die for it, we must acknowledge this good in those who differ from us- we must rejoice that Christ is received. We call this person by that name, and that person by this; but God does not regard the names we may give to this one or that, to this form or that, to this faction or that. He only notices the love, the adoration, the service we show to His Dear Son.'

There was a nobility of disposition about him which ever forbad his meeting any opponent except upon the most open field of controversy or defence. He was too honourable, and his view of a clergyman's course of life was too high in principle, to admit of his countenancing any underground dealings with anyone. Yet he was able to accommodate himself to, and deal in a winning way with, all the various tempers and habits of those to whom he ministered, whether in or out of his church. He was able to go out into the most varying society of the world, coming out unscathed, and having always held his own. It was his rule never to limit himself to one class or party, but to act before all as one who ought to bear about him, as a clergyman of the Church, a sort of *universal character.*

Such was the brave, true, honest, and simple mind which was so misunderstood- almost universally - during life, but which is now as universally acknowledged to be useful far beyond the Church of England.
F. Ernest Tower.

Farewell Address
of the
Rev. F. Ernest Tower, M.A.
to the
Parishioners of Earl's Shilton
ii. Cor. xiii. ii.

"Finally, brethren, farewell. Be perfect, be of good comfort, be of one mind, live in peace; and the God of love and peace shall be with you."

In this text St. Paul directs the Corinthians in a few farewell words to the highest life which they could possibly aim at. I say "aim at," because in the fullest sense "to be perfect as God is perfect," is a state quite unattainable. It was only reached by one, Jesus Christ the Lord. Still, St. Paul would not have thus enjoined them to be "perfect" if perfection in every sense were unattainable. We are therefore bound to believe that whilst there is a perfect perfection which is quite beyond us, there is a perfection out of this perfection which is not only to be aimed at, but attained. With this view of perfection before us, let us take: (1) a retrospective view of this parish looking back twenty-five years, and then (2) an ideal prospective view of the same as it may be realised twenty-five years hence, if good works continue and abound. It is twenty-seven years and more since by God's grace and favour I had the privilege of being instituted the first minister of the new parish. As the steward of God, I am now come to the end of more than a quarter of a century of years of success and of failure, and therefore bound to cast up my accounts, and present them to my heavenly Master. And the natural reflection is, that during that period whilst the sun has shone upon the people, clouds have not been wanting; that whilst joy and pleasure have entered our dwelling places, scarce a house but has been visited by sickness and death; and that sin, the worst enemy of all has been unmistakably followed by judgment upon this and upon that family. I had never heard of Earl's Shilton before Lady Noel Byron (to whom the parish for many previous years was deeply indebted) offered me its cure. And when the first sight of the parish, full of working people, rose upon me, it was only natural that whatever earnestness of mind I possessed should be excited to good works on its behalf. The very thought of such a large population being borne down as they were in those days of low wages and severe trials of one kind and another, seemed to force me to say, "I must do my duty towards these people and they must do their duty to one another. I must act as their counsellor and friend, and they must act as friends to one another; and everything we can do for each other we must do with all good will and heart for God's sake." It was on March 18, 1854 when I set foot in the old impoverished church, and the first person I saw in it was a drunken man. But Christmas had passed, and Lent had begun, and we had encouragement from the Church services which told of the Divine Carpenter, and reminded us that whatever might befall the old edifice - that whatever friend or foe we might find to help or hinder us in doing good, there was One Person we were sure always to find amongst us, and that He could be heartily depended upon - One who would never leave us nor forsake us. It was the Great Head of the Church whom we trusted. And so in His name we, minister and people of that day (assisted largely by the county of Leicester and friends at a distance) set to work to re-build the House of God in which we now so thankfully worship; and afterwards to erect the schools wherein almost a generation of children have been educated. Let me here make a public record of a fact which still redounds to the honour of the population of that day - that in one month of 1854 the people of Earl's Shilton gave their names as subscribers of £600 to the church and schools, and that large sum was eventually paid up almost to the last sovereign. We are apt to speak of poverty now, but poverty now is nothing in comparison of what poverty was then. Ten, twelve and even in a few cases, fifteen hours' work for stocking makers a day, or wages about 7s. or 8s. a week. It cannot be denied that the visible marks of true prosperity were but faintly seen even here and there amongst working people of that day. Read the autobiography of Thomas Cooper, and you will easily understand whether I speak the truth; or read, if you will, the Parliamentary Blue Book of the Framework Knitters Commission, which tells the same tale. The world was hard upon the poor stockingers. Poverty, misery, sin met us again and again in working people's houses. I can remember dwellings where 80 cubic feet of air were all which inmates in some instances had to breathe. Strange standards of merit, too, existed amongst working men. "Liberty, Fraternity, and Equality," was their cry, in the communistic sense. The simple marks of Christian liberty, of the Christian brotherhood of men, and of equality in Christ were but faintly seen. Some working men thought too much of themselves, and became leaders of discontents; and others thought too little of themselves, and loosing self- respect appeared as if bowed down to the very dust. Some in the parish lived unmarried, and yet with children, and these last were turned aside by their parents as ragged children, fit only for the ragged school kept by that honourable old man, William Swinney, the parish clerk. Some lived as if there were neither a heaven by doing well, nor a hell by doing ill. The surface only of religion stood out slightly in relief from the level of ordinary life. At last came the Cotton Famine, and 1,200 people of the village were thrown out of work. A most pitiable time we had of it. But God in His prerogative is moved towards us in our distress, and like the people of Nineveh we heard the rod and who had appointed it. We believed in God, and poverty stricken as we were, we put on sackcloth. Yes, patched sackcloth literally. And we formed monster Bible classes for reading; and the people came just as they were to God's house, and we all felt the keenness of the stroke of privation from the least in the population to the greatest. But, blessed be our Heavenly Guardian and Friend, ever since that date we have been lifted up. - 2. But let me speak to you now of Earl's Shilton in prospect - of the village in the next twenty-five years. You have at this moment excellent schools and a beautiful church. You have better dwelling houses than formerly and better wages. You have most improved village clubs, Co-operative Society, land societies, a coffee house, fairly well regulated public houses, and a generally industrious and well-to-do population, with a kindly spirit amongst you to live socially one with another. You have no longer the old stocking trade in every house, but the shoe trade in great part supplying its place. My friends, these things are good and to be thankful for! You may not all have increased in wealth, but you have grown in good order and respectability. Nevertheless you still require a good shaking - a wholesome shaking out of some of the old ways to which you cling. You want more real Christianity, I mean. I am addressing myself to our working people generally. There is a blank cold want somewhere in the mass of you. There is a void which has not yet been supplied, and which no working man can supply for himself, and which no political faction can supply for him. Brother men and friends - you require something more than trade unions and political combinations. You have struggling aspiring human hearts. You have warm affectionate human natures. You wish to believe in something more than you now believe. You require something that is personal, something that is distinct, something to be vehemently grasped and clung to; and you look into the world and find *nothing that is not wavering and unsteady. You have been, and still are, tempted to make an ideal hero of another working man - a Kossuth, a Ledru Rollin, a Gambetta, an honest John Bright, a Joseph Arch, or, worst of all, a Bradlaugh. Ah, but depend upon it friends, the only Pattern of Patterns, the only centre figure of the world, the only One to make you perfect, is the Son of God, the Divine Man, Jesus of Nazareth, the High Priest of Priests, the Apostle of Apostles, the Second Person of the Eternal Godhead, the grand and dignified and mysterious Being of Love and Goodness, who always stands out in the world quite by Himself, the Divinest of all Divine Characters to the consciousness of believers and unbelievers alike. Would you be perfect in the future? You must study His Life more. Put your trust in Him, the Perfect and Unapproachable One; and then I hope to hear, when I am far removed from you, of your having more of the spirit of true Christianity, the only perfect remedy for all human ills; also of your having more education, and more of the Gospel first, not any new-fangled Gospel, but the old old Gospel that Paul preached when he made tents. You must support your schools well, and your tried school teachers with no niggard hand. You must take care of the house of God, and its sacramental and other services. You must worship here in spirit and in truth. You must remember that not a few favourites merely, but a whole parish are to be saved. And you must listen to proper teaching - none of the baser sort which tends to separate class from class, but that which presents the true brotherhood of men in Christ, and will force you to believe that it is as noble to be a good Christian working man as a good duke and something harder; and that it is in everyone of you, if you try, to be equal with the best, under Him who is the Head over all to the Church which is His Body. So shall Earl's Shilton of the future be a pattern population, a model parish to others. Its Church (not the edifice, but the people) will be a living Church; and its schools will send forth into the world even more, and yet again more young men and women to be a credit to the Christian Church in general and to the village in particular. But everything depends upon the foundation of your characters being Christ, none but Christ - none but Christ! A clearance has to be made in every parishioners heart of pride, envy, malice, and uncharitableness; of intemperance, uncleanness and deceit; of idle and bad words, cursing and swearing; of quarrelsomeness and selfishness, and of all carelessness. For Christ will share with no one who determines to do wrong, a single corner of the foundation stone of the Life in God. Finally, brethren and friends, farewell. Be perfect. Fear God, and no one else. Let your families be pure inside and outside your dwellings. Your young daughters strictly guarded, your young men carefully brought up. Let no clamour or strife have way amongst you, especially in vestry. Let your schools be the best in the entire district, and your little children the patterns of regularity and attention. Let your employers be examples to others in sobriety, temperance, and uprightness. Live all of you above everything mean and dishonourable and shabby in dealings. Study to be quite and orderly, each minding his own business diligently. Be of the same mind. Live in peace. And the God of love and peace shall be with you. In conclusion, let me ask each one here present to make me two promises: 1, That you will read the Bible; if not a whole chapter, at least a few verses, every day. 2, That you will pray for God's blessing upon the new minister who shall come after me. God bless you all.*

With the departure of Tower this fascinating period of village history comes to an end. I believe, however, it would be worthwhile to review and record some subsequent events which took place at Earl Shilton and elsewhere stemming from the Lady Byron and Ernest Tower years, which will be of interest to the reader. It will lead us into the twentieth century; within living memory.

APPENDIX A

The Byron - Tower Legacy

After Lady Byron's death the next person to become Patron of the Living and to hold the manor as a lessee of the Queen was her grandson, Ralph 2nd Earl of Lovelace. On his death in 1906 it appears that no other lessee was appointed, but his widow Lady Lovelace continued as Patroness of the Living until 1920 when the following entry was made in the London Gazette on 31st December in that year:

File no 65896 - Kirkby Mallory R Earl Shilton V & Elmesthorpe R

Transfer of Patronage
Order of His Majesty in Council transferring the patronage of the above mentioned Benefices from the Right Hon. Mary, Countess of Lovelace to the Bishop of Peterborough.

This of course would be passed to the Bishop of Leicester later in the 1920's when the new diocese came into being.

In 1886 the Church received its clock on the spire and in 1923 electric lighting was installed in the Church by the local firm of Messrs.Bray and Coley at a cost of £162-5s-6d.

In 1889 Philip Noel Baker was born who was the great great grandson of the absentee Rector the Rev. Thomas Noel. Philip Noel Baker was a Labour MP and an acknowledged expert on international affairs.

In 1895 the Lord Bishop of Peterborough came to the neighbouring village of Barwell for a Confirmation Service and the following account has survived.

Confirmation Day 1895 - The Earl Shilton candidates assembled at the Vicarage at 1:45pm and at 2pm they started to drive to Barwell in Mr Charlesworth's large brake. When they reached Barwell the bells in the fine old church tower were sending forth their joyous sounds in honour of the visit of the Lord Bishop. The Confirmation Service commenced punctually at 3 o'clock and was a most impressive one. There were twenty four candidates from Earl Shilton viz. twelve females and twelve males. After tea the brake was in readiness, and conveyed the Earl Shilton candidates safely home again.

The Earl Shilton Church Review (Parish Magazine) was distributed from 1922 and The Church of England Mens Society and Mothers Union also commenced at this time when the Rev. H.V. Williams was the vicar. There had been a more basic parish magazine for a number of years before this time.

Problems over the financing of the Church Schools were never far away and many events were organised to raise funds for this purpose. In 1902 Church Schools were eligible to receive support from the local rates.

What happened to the title of Lord Byron? The poet was the 6th Lord and his cousin George Anson Byron was the 7th Lord. No. 8 was a son of the 7th Lord and No.9 was a nephew of the 8th Lord. No. 10 was a brother of the 9th Lord and No.11 was a distant cousin of the 10th Lord and a great grandson of the 7th Lord. Rupert, 11th Lord Byron, was born at Peckleton House in 1903 but after the first World War his parents emigrated to Australia and he followed a few years later becoming a sheep farmer. After service in the Second World War he succeeded to the title in 1949 and died in Australia in 1983. With no heir the title passed to a distant cousin Lt.Colonel Richard Geoffrey Byron and following his recent death his only surviving son Robin became the 13th Lord Byron.

What happened to the Wentworth peerage? The 2nd Viscount Wentworth died in 1815 leaving no heir and this title became extinct. However the title of Baron Wentworth continued and was one of the few titles which could pass to a female. Lady Byron succeeded to this title and in her later years could have used the title of Lady Wentworth. The present holder of the Wentworth peerage is the 5th Earl of Lytton who lives in Sussex and is the great great great grandson of the poet and Lady Byron.

Many of the Tower children, sometimes affectionately referred to locally in the last century as the 'Turretts' returned to Earl Shilton during their lifetime. As previously stated the eldest Henry was Rector of Holy Trinity Church, Windsor 1900-1945 and he returned on several occasions either to preach or attend functions. He attended a three day féte in 1895 accompanied by his brother David and his sister Mary, and returned again on Wake Sunday 29th October 1922 to preach. David was interested in the Scout Movement and Mary presented a number of beautifully embroidered altar cloths and frontals to both the Earl Shilton and Windsor Churches. An article in the Church Review of April 1923 reads as follows:

> We have just received from Miss Mary Tower, a daughter of our first Vicar, a magnificent present to the Church. She has made a set of beautiful altar linen consisting of a Fair Linen Cloth, hand embroidered in handsome designs with four crosses. The 'Ter Sanctus' is embroidered in raised lettering at each end surrounded by tracery and an exquisite chalice veil in superine linen with the sacred monogram in the centre, also a Pall, a linen Corporal and twelve Purificators to match. We are most grateful to Miss Tower for her generosity and thoughtfulness. She has taken infinite care in order that the set should be of the best and accurate in every detail. The set will greatly add to the beauty of the Altar and the well ordering of our services. It will not only be treasured on account of its beauty, usefulness and intrinsic value, but because it will bind us more closely to a family who will ever have an honoured place in the affection of Shiltonians in general and Churchpeople in particular. The linen will be dedicated and used for the first time on Easter Day.

In August 1924 Lieutenant Tower, only son of Henry Tower was drowned at Polperro while on a family holiday and a special muffled peal was rung at Earl Shilton. Henry Tower had two daughters, Cicely and Meriel, and the Church was delighted to welcome Meriel to a Flower Festival on 16th. September 1995. Cicely, who died a few years previously wrote a history of the parish of Windsor. The Rev. Frederick Tower was another son of the Rev. Ernest Tower who returned to Earl Shilton to preach at the Church in the 1920's. On Saturday 3rd. September 1927 members of the Girls' Guild under another long serving teacher, Miss Richardson, visited Windsor Castle. They were welcomed at the Castle Hotel by Henry Tower.

In the 1920's many villagers could claim to have served the Church for a very long time most going back to the days of Tower. In 1927 W.S.Worthy the Sexton and Parish Clerk had completed 64 years as a member of the choir. A grandson of William Swinney, Mr. Worthy was a fine cricketer in his younger days. In July 1878 Earl Shilton played a challenge match against Leicester Town, thought of as the premier club in this area and scored 54 runs, 11 coming from Mr. Worthy. They then proceeded to bowl out Leicester for just 8 runs with Mr. Worthy taking 5 wickets. George Panter played for Earl Shilton in this match. He was at one time landlord of the old Dog and Gun in Keats Lane and a professional cricketer on Leicestershire's books. He was a friendly rival of W.G.Grace.

It is worth digressing for a moment to quote an incident which took place in 1873 concerning Panter and Grace in a match between the United South of England, for whom Grace played, and Leicester and District. In the second innings Leicester required just 43 runs to win. The score stood at 39 for nine wickets with Panter on 19 not out and about to face the next over from G.F.Grace the brother of W.G. The story goes that Grace had made a bet of £5 with another person that Panter would not score 20 runs in this second innings, and before his brother bowled the over they had a few words with one another. What followed was that G.F.Grace bowled a wide which went to the boundary giving Leicester victory but leaving Panter stranded on 19 not out- and of course Grace won his bet. Many of the large crowd were convinced that this had been done deliberately and expressed their disapproval.

The brothers D. and R. Loxley had both completed nearly 60 years in the choir, while the former had been organist for 50 years. Mr. Sam Coe had served in the choir for 40 years and was another of Earl Shilton's professional cricketers having scored a record score of 252 not out for Leicestershire against Northants in 1914. Mr. E.H. Gilbert had been Vicar's Warden for 25 years, and Mr. James Metcalfe who had taken over from Mr. Reynolds as headmaster of the schools at the turn of the century had also completed 25 years.

Mr. Worthy by his will bequeathed a sum of money to be used for two stained glass windows for the south side of the Church, stipulating that the work must be carried out by Kempe & Co. renowned for their workmanship. The principal partner in the firm of Kempe was at this time Mr. Walter E. Tower the youngest son of the Rev. Ernest Tower.

At the close of the year 1921 the Rev. G.A. Studdert Kennedy visited the church and preached to a capacity congregation. He was better known by his nickname of 'Woodbine Willie' acquired from the practical and spiritual help he gave to the soldiers in the Great War.

In common with other places of worship Earl Shilton Church in the 1920's supported a football team in the Hinckley and District Sunday School League, a Church Girls Hockey Club and encouraged many other sporting activities. Church outings, too, were very popular in the 1920's and it is worth recording in this book the reports written by usually the secretary of the group involved even if it is only to ensure their survival. Fragile vanished memories seem to become fresh again in such accounts.

Church of England Men's Society Annual Outing To Shakespeare Country June 1926

Dark, dismal, lowering clouds could not damp the bright spirits of the members of C.E.M.S. who assembled at the Schools at noon on Saturday, June 12th., for their visit to the world-famed town of Stratford-on-Avon. Mr. Edwards' comfortable and commodious chara was soon loaded, and the party set off shortly after 12 o'clock. It was noticed that certain members were specially equipped for the journey with special hats and goggles. Just after crossing the Watling Street, a heavy shower compelled a halt, when after considerable struggling, the covers were put up, and the journey continued. Past Wolvey and Shilton the rain was forgotten as prospects of the Test match were discussed. Mr. Edwards took the road right through the centre of Coventry, giving the party an opportunity of glimpses of that famous city. Arrived at Guys Cliffe a halt was made where many took advantage of the chance of visiting the famous old Saxon Mill, and also of admiring the weir and the lovely view of Guy's Cliffe House, now in possession of the Percy family. In glorious sunshine Stratford was reached shortly before three. Members dispersed in groups, some enjoying the sights and beauties revealed by a river trip whilst others visited the Church and the various places connected with England's most famous poet. An excellent tea was provided at the quaint old Shakespeare Cafe, where such modern inventions as electric light looked strangely out of place in its Elizabethan surroundings. Tea concluded, the Vicar presided over a brief but pleasing ceremony, when Mr. Grewcock, the President, presented a pouch and tobacco to Mr. Warr, the indefatigable Secretary, from the brothers, as a small token of their regard for his services.

After a short time allowed for sightseeing, Stratford was left at 7 p.m. for Leamington. With the top down, a beautiful evening sun, this ride among the leafy Warwickshire lanes, with the foliage clean washed by the morning showers, was one of the most enjoyable features of the day. A short stay at Leamington enabled members to visit the beautiful Jephson Gardens, and also taste the 'sweet' waters for which the town is so famous. Leamington was left about nine o'clock, and again the ride was much enjoyed. The journey was enlivened by the musical efforts of some of the brothers, and great hilarity was caused when Mr. Edwards was stopped at lighting-up time, by one of the brothers who was exceedingly anxious to know whether the driver had provided himself with the necessary red oil for his rear light. The Schools were reached shortly before eleven, and the party dispersed after one of the most enjoyable outings the Society had ever had. An amusing incident occurred as the village was reached. Various members alighted near their homes, and considerable wonder was caused by one brother who alighted at the telephone office though his home was not in its immediate vicinity. A solution was found by the brother of ' red oil' fame, who gravely informed the company that the brother who had just alighted wished to telephone to his family the fact of his safe arrival.

The Mothers' Excursion to London- July 1923
Written by a Mother

Well, I am just alive after our expedition to London, and the Vicar got over 60 mothers to London and back without losing one. It was a day ! We started off, packed like sardines in a motor bus at 7-30 a.m. At Elmesthorpe two picnic saloons awaited us and into them we jumped. At Rugby 62 cups of good tea were in readiness for us, and right glad we were for a cup, some of us had had but little breakfast, we were too excited to eat.

We arrived at Euston (after criticising the London washing en route) at 11 a.m. and two buses welcomed us, then off we went to St. Paul's, we were held up many times by the traffic which was terrific! At St. Paul's we had a special permit from the Dean and a special verger to take us round, down into the crypt we descended and walked among the tombs of Nelson, Wellington, Roberts and the illustrious dead. Wellington's funeral carriage being especially interesting. Well, you would have smiled to see the Vicar hustling the sporting mothers, all keen as mustard, to see and hear everything and staggering, panting along. tall and thin, short and portly, all were hustled. We were told we must keep to the scheduled time ! " Now come along!" " Jump on this bus!" "If you were on top last time you must get inside this time !" "Anyone late will be left behind !!! " and as some had never been in London before and were not a little alarmed, this was an awful threat. The two bus conductors were very popular, very loquacious and very facetious.

From St. Paul's we were driven along the Embankment, through Trafalgar Square, across Piccaddily Circus to 'Maison Lyons' in Regent Street, where we had an excellent dinner, well served - Fish, roast beef, Yorkshire pudding, new potatoes, cabbage and plum tart. During the journey up a collection had been made in order to purchase some flowers for the Cenotaph, so one of the mothers after dinner dashed off and bought a bunch of splendid Iris. At 1-30 we mounted the vehicles once again, or to be correct, all did except one, who was seen in the middle of Regent Street calmly holding up the traffic until a head poked out of a taxi window and said : "Don't you know that you are in a little country town called London?" A reverent halt was made at the Cenotaph whilst our bunch of flowers was placed in position, attached to the flowers was a card inscribed " In memory of the brave who died for us - From the Earl Shilton Mothers' Union." Then on we went to the M.U.Headquarters, where we toiled three flights of stairs and saw very little, however, we did our duty and called at our Headquarters. The stairs proved too much for some of us, and consequently little drops of water had to be dispersed, on to Westminster Abbey we went, where some half a dozen dropped on the chairs, totally unable to keep up any longer ! The still determinedly energetic ones went round with a guide and the weary ones waited anxiously for a sight of the party again, fearing they might disappear through another door ! From thence we went to the House of Lords where we were greeted by both Major and Mrs. Guy Paget. We were shown the Throne Room and Princes Chamber and even the Gilded Chamber itself. One mother thought the carpet around the two thrones a bit shabby ! We saw the various Lobbies and the Lobby to the House of Commons was like a fair, much shouting out of names and much running to and fro. We walked along the glorious terrace and saw Mrs. Wintringham, one of the three lady members. A visit to St. Stephens Chapel was most interesting. Tea was served in a room overlooking the Terrace, over which Mrs. Paget presided. Major Paget was very kind and pleasant to us all. He possesses a keen sense of quiet humour and I heard him remark to a fellow member as he was following a flock of 63 mothers, " I have one or two friends to tea to-day!"

After tea the Vicar thanked Major and Mrs. Paget for their kindness and both responded in such a gracious manner.

The Policemen on duty were rather amused with the whole proceeding, one said that they were the happiest lot he had seen for a long time.

After a desperate hustle across the street we boarded our buses, thence on to Buckingham Palace, Hyde Park, Marble Arch, Oxford Street to 'Selfridges'. It was Alexandra Day so London (bathed in glorious sunshine) looked pretty and festive with roses. We arrived at Selfridges and went up in lifts to the Tea Room where another sumptuous meal was provided, but after such a lovely tea at the House of Commons we hardly did justice to it and also we were simply longing to do a bit of shopping. Up and down stairs or in lifts we went, along corridors and down passages beseeching attendants to tell us where the blouse department was or the toy department or whichever counter we sought most of all. Oh ! it was so bewildering ! We must have walked miles in Selfridges. Some members of our party spent their time having joy rides or otherwise in the lifts, not knowing which floor they wanted, others were found stranded outside lifts and hauled in or hauled out and landed on terra ferma. Six o'clock was the appointed hour to be ready to depart in the buses for Euston, and the time came, but only 40 were present, search was hurriedly made for the miscreants and when admonished they said it wasn't because they wanted to be late but because they couldn't find their way out of Selfridges. After a harassing and hair-raising ten minutes, we started a John Gilpin ride to Euston and we just caught our train with only two minutes to spare, and when our Vicar counted us he found to his great relief that no one was left behind.

At Nuneaton, the secretary, Mrs. S.Norton, on behalf of the party, presented the Vicar with a fine box of choice cigarettes. I suppose to steady his nerves after what must have been to him an anxious day.

Lads' Bible Class Outing to London June 1926
(By one of the Lads)

A most enjoyable day was spent in London by the members of the Lads' Bible Class, accompanied by the Vicar and Mr. Grewcock. We left home just before 8 o'clock and arrived in London just after 11 o'clock. On arriving in London we went by the Underground to Westminster, and then walked past the Cenotaph to the Houses of Parliament, where the party were met by Miss Tower (daughter of the late Rev. E.Tower, of Earl Shilton). At the Houses of Parliament eight acres of ground were covered, and the various sights were greatly enjoyed. We then crossed Whitehall and had a walk round the Abbey, where the Unknown Warrior's grave was seen. By this time most of the boys were feeling rather peckish, so an enjoyable dinner was partaken of at the Abbey Restaurant. We next proceeded by foot to Trafalgar Square, and from there by 'bus to the Zoo via Regent Street, which has recently been rebuilt. At the Zoo we had a fine time, and great interest was taken in the exhibits, especially in the bird houses and the aquarium. The white elephant which had recently arrived was seen. Tea was taken at the Zoo, and after that the reptile houses were visited. We left the Zoo at 6 o'clock and returned to Trafalgar Square by 'bus. Then a walk was taken along the Thames Embankment, St. Paul's being seen in the distance. The Savoy Hotel was passed and also 2LO, a building of interest to wireless enthusiasts, and we wended our way to ' The Coliseum.' On the way to this place of amusement one small boy lost the cherries which he had bought to eat there. Arrived at the Coliseum the show was greatly enjoyed, and the most interesting items being the Jazz Band and also Miss Betty Blythe. After the show we adjourned to Lyon's Corner House for supper, after which we went back to the station by underground, and got there with a few minutes to spare. Most of us tried to go to sleep coming home, but it was of no avail. After a good journey we arrived in Leicester just after 2 o'clock, where Vernon Bros.' 'bus was waiting to carry us home, and tired but happy we reached home just about 3 a.m.

Girls' Guild Outing 1927

On Saturday, Sept 3rd., members and friends of the Girls' Guild, accompanied by the Vicar, had a delightful day's outing to Windsor and Hampton Court. The party left Earl Shilton by Red 'bus for Leicester, and there took a train for London. Arriving at

St. Pancras at 10 a.m., charas were waiting to convey the party to Windsor. Before visiting the Royal Castle lunch was partaken of at the Castle Hotel, where the Rev. Tower was a guest of the party. The tour of the Castle and the grounds was full of interest to all. The State Apartments, sumptuously furnished and enriched by an historical collection of works of art, and the visit to the cloisters, gateways, terraces, etc., impressed the party of the grandeur of this Royal Castle, and also how closely connected it is with our national history. From Windsor the party motored to Hampton Court, where the beauty of the gardens will be remembered by all. Tea was served at the Thames Hotel, and then reluctantly the party commenced the return journey via Richmond and many interesting parts of London. At midnight the tourists reached home, very tired but enthusiastic over the visit to the Royal Palaces.

Great credit is due to Miss Richardson, the President of the Girls' Guild, for all the excellent arrangements made for the outing. After tea the Vicar, on behalf of the Girls' Guild, thanked Miss Richardson for all she had done to make the party so happy and joyous, and hoped she would be blessed with health and strength to continue her good work with the Guild for many years.

Children's Outing to Skegness 1927

Thursday, August 11th., was a great day for the children of Earl Shilton, two or three hundred of whom spent a very enjoyable day by the sea. Altogether (including parents) about 340 made the journey, travelling to Leicester in nine Red 'buses and thence by rail to Skegness, where a happy day was spent patronising various amusements or on the sands. Lunch was taken with them and partaken of on the train, and an excellent tea was also provided at the Pavilion Tower Gardens. Many of the children had paid into a special fund since the beginning of the year and thus were not only able to pay expenses, but also had a surplus to spend at the seaside. The Vicar (Rev. E. Pillifant) accompanied the party, and those children whose parents were unable to go, were under his wing. They each wore "identification discs" bearing their name and the name of the party together with the time of the return train, so that the risk of any being lost was reduced to a minimum; and it is believed that all returned safely to their homes, arriving in Earl Shilton just before midnight. The event, which was the first of the kind, was held to arouse interest in the work of the Sunday Schools.

On Sunday evening 16th March 1924 the Vicar the Rev. H.V. Williams gave a religious address on the radio from the B.B.C. in Birmingham. At this time B.B.C. stood for the British Broadcasting Company as the Corporation was not formed until 1926. Reports stated that his voice came through loud and clear and those few people in the parish who possessed radio sets had a full house.

As a reflection of the changing conditions in the parish from the arrival of Tower in 1854, until 1927 when many still remembered him and his family at the Vicarage, there were nineteen married couples living in the village who had celebrated their golden wedding having been married during Tower's curacy and this fact was recorded in the National Press:

Through the generosity of Mr. A.H.Bradbury, those couples of Earl Shilton who had been fortunate enough to live to celebrate their golden wedding were entertained to tea at 'Hollydene' the home of Mr. Bradbury on Wednesday. The event, unique in the history of Earl Shilton and probably of Leicestershire created a great deal of interest in the district for nineteen couples had been invited for the occasion and happily the majority were able to attend.

The names of those present were:

Mr. & Mrs. Sharpe, Spring Gardens.
Mr. & Mrs. S. Taylor, Church Street.
Mr. & Mrs. Smith, Hill Top Farm.
Mr. & Mrs. J. Mays, Hill Top Farm.
Mr. & Mrs. J. Foster, Keats Lane.
Mr. & Mrs. W. Faulks, High Street.
Mr. G. Foster, Almeys Lane (Wife absent)
Mr. & Mrs. C. Thompson, The Barracks.
Mr. T. Toon, Council Houses, (Wife absent)
Mr. & Mrs. J. Faulks, Station Road.
Mr. & Mrs. D. Pick, Wood Street.
Mr. & Mrs. J. Tebbut, Highfield Street.
Mr. & Mrs. A. Breward, Land Society.
Mr. & Mrs. Down, Station Road.
Mr. & Mrs. R. Cockerill, Church Street.
Mr. & Mrs. S. Barratt, 41, New Street.
Mr. & Mrs. James Colver, Almeys Lane.
Mr. Thomas Marvin, wife absent and no address given.

The combined ages of these long married ladies and gentlemen aggregated 2767 years at an average age of 72.8. The oldest persons present were Mr. J. Mays (82) and Mr. T. Toon (80). Great pleasure was exhibited by the happy couples when at tea a message from the King and Queen, which had arrived early in the afternoon in reply to a telegram sent to their Majesties on their behalf was read to them. It read:

'The King and Queen sincerely thank the nineteen golden wedding couples of Earl Shilton assembled today for their loyal message of greeting. Their Majesties send their cordial good wishes to all who are taking part in the remarkable gathering and trust that they are enjoying the best of health.'

After tea which was enlivened by music provided over the wireless by means of a portable set installed by Mr. Clarence Goode of Hinckley, congratulatory speeches were the order.

It is sad to recall that the Vicarage built by Tower was demolished in 1956, and the schools erected by him were closed and transferred to more modern buildings in the 1980's and 90's. The Church of St. Simon & St. Jude however remains as a memorial to this respected man who arrived here by courtesy of Lady Byron. The early 1950's saw the demolition also of three famous houses mentioned in this book - Kirkby Mallory Hall, Gopsall Hall and the Tower family home Weald Hall in Essex, all three being a great loss to the heritage of the country. As a final blow the rectory at Kirkby Mallory fell victim to damp and dry rot and other infestations, in spite of many attempts to save it and it was finally demolished a few years ago. I hope that this book can preserve some of that history which these buildings represented.

SUGGESTED FURTHER READING

History of Earl Shilton and Tooley Park by G.H.Foster 1947.
The Real Lady Byron by Joan Pierson. Robert Hale, London 1992
Byron: A Portrait by Leslie A.Marchand. John Murray, London 1971
Byron's Letters and Journals by Leslie A.Marchand. John Murray, London 1973-82
Ada, Countess of Lovelace by Doris Langley Moore. John Murray, London 1977.
The Noels and the Milbankes by Malcolm Elwin. Macdonald & Co. London 1967
Lord Byron's Wife by Malcolm Elwin. Macdonald & Co. London 1962
Re-issued by John Murray, London 1974
Lord Byron's Family by Malcolm Elwin. John Murray, London 1975.
Byron and The Romantics in Switzerland 1816 by Elma Dangerfield. Ascent Books, London 1978 and Thomas Lyster Ltd. Ormskirk, 1992.
Life and Letters of Frederick W.Robertson. M.A. Smith, Elder & Co. London 1866.
The Byron Women by Margot Strickland, Peter Owen, London, 1974.

APPENDIX B

A Guide to The Parish Church of St. Simon & St. Jude, Earl Shilton, Leics.

COMPILED BY MR. JOHN GILBERT AND MR. JOE LAWRANCE

Proceeding around the Church on the suggested route shown in the plan overleaf:

The Children's Corner
Near to the main entrance - was formed in the early 1980's. In front of it is the old Parish Chest which dates from before 1550. In 1538 King Henry VIII decreed that all parishes should record every Christening, Wedding and Burial, and that these records be kept in a strong chest with two locks. In 1597 this was increased to three locks.

The Tower
This is the oldest part of the Church, housing a fine ring of eight bells, the oldest three dating from 1606, 1612 and 1711. Two more were added in 1875 making five, rung from the ground floor. All were re-cast in 1921 by Taylors of Loughborough and three more were added, one being in honour of the 1,000 men from the village who served the colours in the First World War, 1914-1918. The Church has maintained a tradition of a good band of ringers who have won many awards for good striking, together with an excellent band of handbell ringers.

PLAN OF THE PARISH CHURCH OF ST SIMON AND ST JUDE, EARL SHILTON

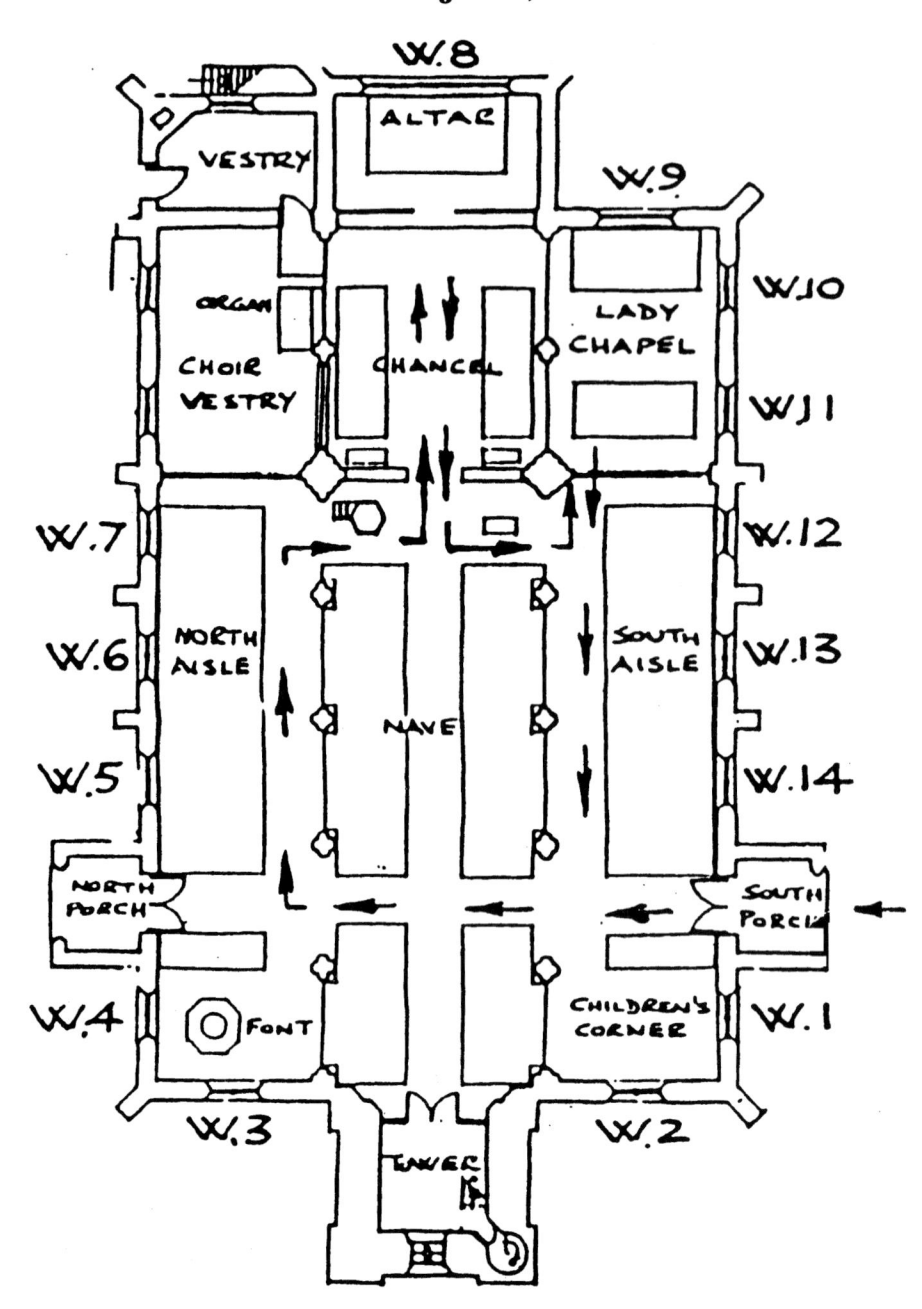

(The windows are designated W1-W14)

The Font
This is often found by the main entrance to a Church, as the first sight on entering (as Baptism is the first Ceremony in life). Here it is seen near the North Door - which was originally used as the main entrance.

The Windows
Of the eight stained glass windows, four are by C.E. Kempe & Co. Ltd. Charles Eamer Kempe was born in 1837 and founded the firm which became famous, producing over 4,000 windows between 1895 and 1934. These windows were often identified by a wheatsheaf (from his Coat of Arms) in the bottom left corner. On Kempe's death in 1907 the firm continued with Walter Tower (a relative of our first vicar) as Chairman and from that time - as will be seen - a black tower (from the name of the Chairman) was placed in the centre of the wheatsheaf.

Window W.6
A Kempe window, featuring on the left St. Simon and on the right St. Jude.

The Pulpit
The carving is by Mrs. Fulshaw, wife of Dr. Fulshaw (village G.P. and Churchwarden) in 1901 and bears the inscription 'Blessed are they that hear the Word of God and keep it. Luke xi.xxviii'.

The Arch
Leading from the Nave to the Chancel bears - top centre - the symbols

IC	XC
NI	KA

This is the Greek translation of 'Jesus Christ Conquers'.
(IC - 'Jesus', XC - 'Christos', NIKA - 'Conquers' 'C' being the Capital version of 'Sigma')

The Chancel
The fine woodwork and carving of the Choirstalls, Chairs, panels around the Altar, and the screens to the Lady Chapel are all the work of craftsmen in the firm of Warren Stanger, Leicester, during the period 1948 - 1956. Mrs. Stanger was first cousin of E.H. Gilbert (Window W.12). The Choirstalls are to the memory of all who served in the Second World War, 1939 - 1945.

The Chancel Carpet
Was made by Mrs. Archer and her daughters in 1930. When completed, they wheeled it to the Church on a bicycle from their remote cottage, between Watery Gate and Croft Hill.

The Organ
Built by Taylors of Leicester in 1933, (replacing the original organ, used from 1875) this has been renovated in 1963 and 1993 additional stops being added on both occasions.

The Decoration
On the Chancel ceiling and walls was by the Rev. Ernest Tower, first vicar. His stencilling covered all the walls and central arches until 1959 when some parts of the exterior walls were affected by damp and it was found that the original damp-proof course had been covered. Part of this decoration on the Sanctuary Walls - either side of the East Window (W.8) - includes the Star of David, together with the Alpha and Omega, the 'First and Last' used in the Book of Revelations as the title of Jesus Christ who, as the Word of God, is the beginning and end of all creation. The other symbol, a letter 'P' surmounting a letter 'X' represents 'Christ the King' (the letter 'X' in Greek being equivalent to 'CH' and the Greek letter 'P' being equivalent to 'R' - i.e. 'Christus Rex').

The Sanctuary (containing the Altar)
The main, beautiful East Window (W.8) above the Altar originally had stained glass just in the three centre lights by an unknown artist, installed about 1884. They depict the ascending Christ with the eleven disciples watching. The two outer lights and tracery were by Morris & Co. and date from 1925. That on the left depicts The Holy Family and above, the Archangel Gabriel with Lily and Staff. That on the right depicts The Last Supper and above, the Archangel Raphael with Martyr's Palm. The row of five rounded windows above depict, from left to right, St. Matthew (Winged Man), St. Mark (Winged Lion), Angel (Holding Crown), St. Luke (Winged Ox) and St. John (Eagle).

The Lectern
In the form of an eagle spreading it's wings. This was given by Dr. Garrett (Village G.P. after Dr. Fulshaw and prior to Dr. Cook) in memory of his wife, in 1924.

The Lady Chapel
Was formed in 1923, the East Window (W.9) by Kempe, being a memorial to those who died in the First World War 1914 - 1918. Each side are panels bearing the names of all from the Parish who gave their lives in both World Wars. The centre light depicts St. Michael plunging a spear into a dragon (the Devil). That on the left depicts St. Nicholas, patron saint of children, wearing a Bishop's Mitre, and on the right is St. George with sword and lance wearing a cloak. For many years at Sunday School 'Sermons' a high sloping platform was constructed covering the whole of the Lady Chapel and the first seven pews, on which all the children were seated. To the right of the window is an 'Ambry' (or 'Aumbry') in which are kept portable Communion vessels to take to the sick and infirm. This is in memory of Dr. James Cook, Village G.P. for over 50 years and Churchwarden for 33 years.

Window W.10
By Jones & Willis depicting on the left Christ teaching in the Temple with worshippers, and on the right, Jews and Priests. In the tracery is a half figure of St. Simon with saw and fish.

Window W.11
By Jones & Willis. The text 'Suffer little children to come unto me'. Half figure of St. Jude with ship.

Window W.12
By J. Wippell & Co. Ltd. (Artist G. Cooper - Abbs). On the left an Angel holding a sacred heart and on the right, Christ in Majesty with Martyr's palm.

Window W.13
By Kempe depicting on the left St. Augustine and on the right St. Ambrose - two of the great Latin doctors of the Church.

Window W.14
By Kempe depicting on the left St. Peter, Apostle and on the right St. Paul, Apostle.

Board
Showing list of Incumbents. This is in memory of H. William Gilbert (Churchwarden 1937 - 1945) and his wife.

Incumbents

18th March 1854	Ferdinand Ernest Tower
10th March 1882	Theodore Calliphronas
17th May 1883	Robert Walter Churchill Hamilton
7th November 1884	John Thomas Willis
24th May 1892	James Slade Maughan
15th July 1921	Herbert Victor Williams
15th December 1926	Edmund Pillifant
17th April 1943	Eynon Edryd Cyndeirne Jones
14th September 1948	Alec Tewkesbury
5th May 1954	Alfred Reginald Ennis
11th September 1956	George Jager
14th June 1968	Alfred Edgar Taylor
11th August 1983	Norman Hulme
9th November 1989	Graham Gittings

Earl Shilton's rebuilt church dedicated to St. Simon and St. Jude

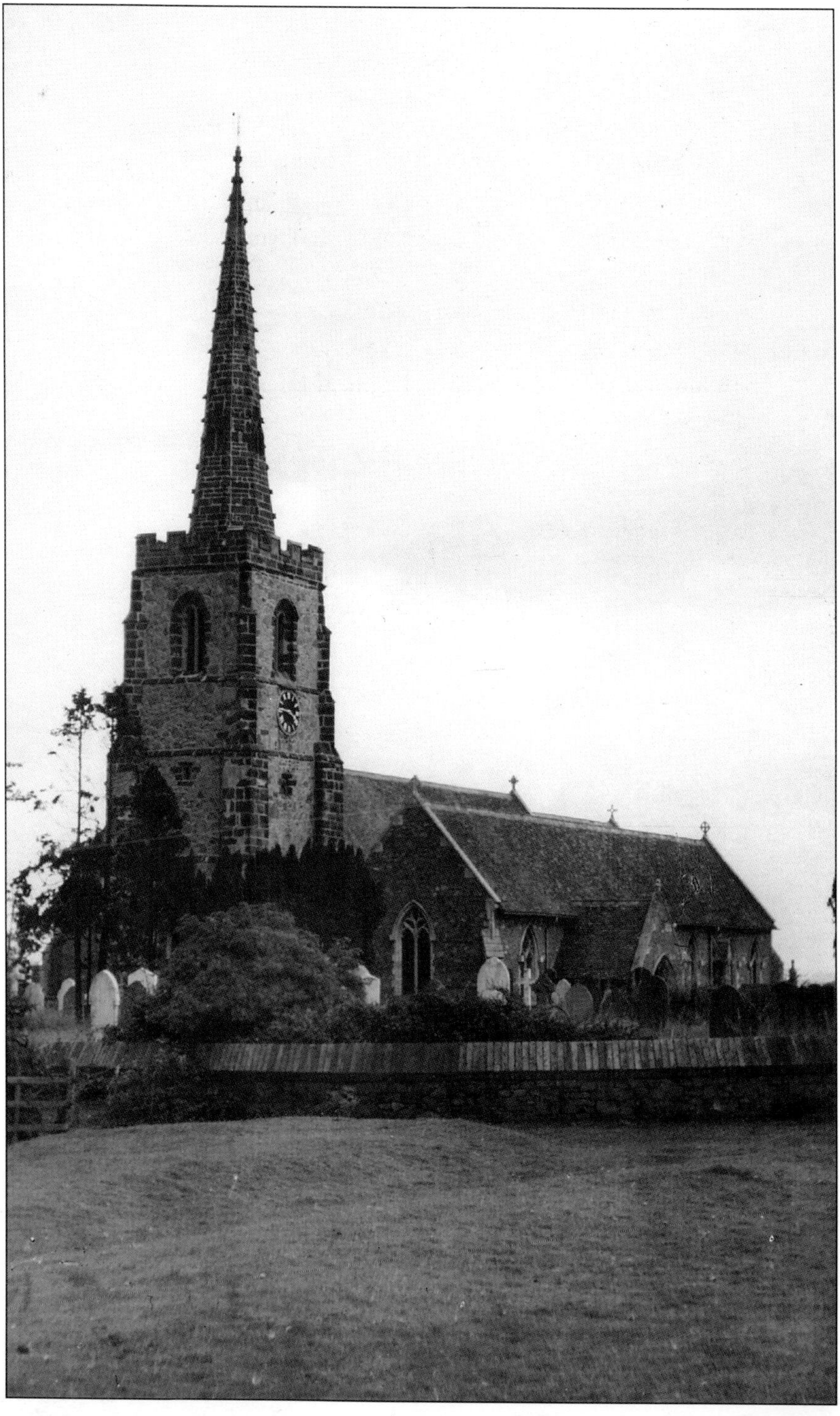